HOUSES
AND HOMES

The Nearby History Series
David E. Kyvig, *Series Editor*
Myron A. Marty, *Consulting Editor*

ML.2

Houses
and Homes

Exploring Their History

Barbara J. Howe, Dolores A. Fleming,
Emory L. Kemp, and Ruth Ann Overbeck

The American Association for State and Local History
Nashville, Tennessee

Library of Congress Cataloging-in-Publication Data

Houses and homes.

  (The Nearby history series)
  Includes bibliographies and index.
  1. United States—History, Local—Handbook, manuals, etc. 2. Dwellings—United States—
Historiography. 3. Historic buildings—United States. 4. Local history.
I. Howe, Barbara J.   II. Series.
E180.H68 1987   973   87-1404
ISBN 0-910050-84-8

Cover design by Gillian Murrey

Contents

Editors' Introduction

COMMUNITIES WITHOUT UNDERSTANDINGS OF THEIR PASTS resemble people suffering from amnesia, unable to remember from where they came, how they responded to needs or challenges, from whence they drew affection and support, or opposition, and where they intended to go. History, the contemplation and evaluation of the past, serves society much as memory serves the individual in identifying circumstances, providing a guide to satisfactory behavior, and offering a standard of comparison across time and situation. In this sense, history is far more than a remembrance of things past, though it certainly includes that. History represents a means of coming to terms with the past, of developing an awareness of previous influences, current conditions, and future possibilities. Just as memory helps the individual avoid having to repeat the same discoveries, behaviors, and mistakes, historical knowledge helps the community avoid starting at the beginning each time it addresses an issue.

History, in addition to being useful, is accessible. Any literate person can pursue and master most historical research techniques as well as historical explanations. Furthermore, history is interesting. Whether reading other people's mail, understanding how ordinary people lived their everyday lives at other times and in other places, or assessing how institutions rose or decayed, the individual studying history constantly finds exciting opportunities to learn about the human condition.

All of these values of history hold as true for the nearby world as for the larger sphere. English historian H. P. R. Finberg considered "the family, the local community, the national state, and the supra-national society as a series of concentric circles." He observed, "Each requires to be studied with constant reference to the one outside it; but the inner rings are not the less perfect circles for being wholly surrounded and enclosed by the outer." In fact, understanding the history of the world close at hand is of great value, for it is this history that shapes the circumstances we all must deal with directly and constantly.

In 1982 we wrote a book that professed the importance of taking a look at the history of the close-at-hand world and attempted to provide assistance in so doing. *Nearby History: Exploring the Past around You* was by design merely an introduction to a broad and complex topic. The book raised questions for consideration, pointed out the sorts of materials that exist for historical research, suggested generally how they might be used, and indicated some of the published work on nearby historical topics that might offer useful models or comparisons. *Nearby History* was predicated on the belief that useful inquiry into the nearby past was not an undertaking for academic professionals alone, but could be pursued in a worthwhile fashion by interested students or out-of-school adults. We intended to stir interest and to indicate how local concerns could comfortably mesh with sophisticated historical thinking.

Growing interest in the subjects and objectives addressed in *Nearby History* has persuaded us that a need exists for a series of books focused on specific aspects of the close-at-hand world. Particular issues and institutions in the community deserving historical consideration pose individual problems of research and analysis. Schools, homes, churches, businesses, and public places are among the nearby world's features that deserve to be addressed historically, each in its own way. The volumes in the "Nearby History" series will give outstanding specialists in these areas the opportunity to guide readers engaged in their own local investigations.

Houses and Homes: Exploring Their History, by Barbara J. Howe, Dolores A. Fleming, Emory L. Kemp, and Ruth Ann Overbeck, is an important volume in this series. After all, communities are often characterized by the living arrangements of their members. Places of residence shape the lives of their occupants and define the nature and functioning of the community. Historians of the nearby world can profit from understanding both the biographies of individual homes and the influences that determined local housing patterns.

In this book, Howe and her colleagues provide a guide to resources needed to examine the design and history of residential structures in the first part. In the second part, they show how to relate the building itself to its environment. The final chapter is a condensed house history demonstrating how research techniques can be blended with knowledge of historical trends to document a building. As their title implies, the authors are reminding historians to consider not only the structures called "houses," but also the centers of human activity called "homes." The authors combine experience in social, cultural, and technological history, engineering, historic preservation, teaching, and contract research. The stimulating questions they raise suggest how to use a variety of helpful research methods and materials and call attention to interesting approaches and conclusions by other historians. Because numerous books already document building styles and advise those rehabilitating old buildings, the authors concentrate on presenting research techniques and, most critically, on providing a research framework for house historians. Their extensive bibliographies help researchers pursue a wide variety of specialized topics. *Houses and Homes* shows readers how to undertake interesting and worthwhile explorations of a past that has great meaning for their own lives.

DAVID E. KYVIG, Series Editor
MYRON A. MARTY, Consulting Editor

Illustrations

THE AUTHORS AND PUBLISHER WISH TO THANK THE FOL-
lowing individuals and organizations for granting permission to reproduce,
on the pages listed below, pictorial material from their collections.

Armstrong World Industries, p. 36
Assiginack Historical Museum, p. 64
The Bancroft Library, p. 31
Cincinnati Historical Society, pp. 87 and 88
Dennett, Muessig, Ryan & Assoc. Ltd. and the U.S. Army Corps of
    Engineers—Huntington District, pp. 70 and 71
Jan Kristin Engel, p. 90
William Fink, National Park Service, pp. 27 and 29
Robert Gamble, Alabama Historical Commission, p. 43
Leonard Grimes, p. 11
Robert J. Hughes, pp. 16, 49, 54, 60, 63, 66, 121, and 151
Richard Lucier, p. 83
Harold Mansfield, p. 73
Allen G. Noble and the University of Massachusetts Press, p. 98
Elizabeth Nolin, pp. 101, 111, 114, 119, and 122
Gladys J. Overbeck, cover
Sears, Roebuck and Co., pp. 84, 128, 131
Temple University Press and George McDaniel, pp. 141 and 142
John Wiley & Sons, Inc., pp. 114, 119, and 122
All other photograhs are from the authors' personal collections.

Acknowledgments

THIS BOOK WAS A JOINT ENDEAVOR EVERY STEP ALONG THE way, so our list of people to acknowledge is long. To those who supplied illustrations (Alabama Historical Commission; Armstrong World Industries; Assiginack Historical Museum; Bancroft Library of the University of California—Berkeley; Cincinnati Historical Society; Dennett, Muessig, Ryan & Assoc., Ltd.; William Fink; Leonard Grimes; Donald Hemmann; Robert J. Hughes; Emory L. Kemp; Richard Lucier; Harold Mansfield; George McDaniel; Allen G. Noble; Sears, Roebuck and Co.; and Temple University Press; to Gladys J. Overbeck, who provided the cover photograph; to Elizabeth Nolin for preparing the drawings of construction materials and regional housing; to Jina Bissett and all the staff of the West Virginia University Department of History and Program in the History of Science and Technology for providing secretarial support; to the staff members of the WVU Communications Service for their assistance in copying photographs; and to David Kyvig, Myron Marty, and Candace Floyd for their editorial assistance, patience, counsel, and support—we owe a big thank you.

We also thank the students in the various historic preservation classes at West Virginia University and Heidelberg College who "tried out" this manuscript in draft stages, shared their research on historic buildings, or helped refine our techniques for teaching the history of housing; the staff of the National Trust for Historic Preservation library who assisted with the bibliography; Austin Beall and the many Manitoulin Island residents who assisted us in gaining an understanding of their history; Dr. K. Doherty and the staff of the Timmins Museum in Timmins, Ontario, for research assistance; and to Melissa McLoud of the American Studies Department of The George Washington University and the staff of the Montana Historical Society for research assistance.

Also, thanks to those who reviewed parts of the manuscript in various drafts: Robert T. Howe, professor emeritus of civil engineering at the University of Cincinnati; Barbara Caron, former director of the Morgantown, West Virginia, Public Library; Allen G. Noble of the Department of Geography, University of Akron; Lizbeth Pyle of the WVU Department of Geology and Geography; the staff of Friendship Hill National Historic Site; and Donald Johnson of the Department of History, Flinders University, Adelaide, South Australia. Most important, however, this book would not exist without the endless support provided by our staunchest partners in this endeavor—William W. Fleming, Robert J. Hughes, and Janet K. Kemp.

BARBARA J. HOWE
DOLORES A. FLEMING
EMORY L. KEMP
RUTH ANN OVERBECK

HOUSES
AND HOMES

·1·

Why Explore a Home's History?

"THE STRENGTH OF A NATION LIES IN THE HOMES OF its people," said Abraham Lincoln. A place to live and the activity within that space, the home life, play an important role in the lives of Americans. Therefore, there are many reasons to investigate the history of a house. One is that it is simply fun to do. What starts out as a trip back into the history of a house can lead to an investigation of a neighborhood and to a systematic survey of the area, to educational programs, or to public relations plans with a historical slant. The research may even be undertaken in order to write a story to be presented as a gift.

Research into the history of housing can illustrate many aspects of American social history. One could learn, for example, about the lives of eighteenth-century mothers in slave quarters or late-twentieth-century professionals with home offices. One could trace the decline of ethnic identity in a community that no longer builds homes in the traditional way or measure the social status of a neighborhood by its adoption of indoor plumbing and two-car garages. Research into the reasons a family farm was subdivided into suburban tracts could reveal the relative profitability of agriculture and the pressures of suburbanization. One could study how the government's destruction of small-scale housing in an old section of the city resulted in the development of high-rise public housing projects. A study of public housing could also show a social worker's view of "acceptable" residents or the building technology that made high-rise structures possible. Research could reflect how some suburban developments followed garden city theories of community planning—theories that have been enforced through building permits, subdivision regulations, and deed restrictions.

House history research combines several skills and cuts across several disciplines. Genealogists are house historians when they trace a building only for the time a particular family lived there. Genealogical research techniques are routinely used by house historians. For example, one may find that a group of similar houses was actually built by members of the same family. House historians also use local history research skills, such as gathering oral history and interpreting maps, photographs, and written records. They also draw on the fields of building technology, architectural history, and geography.

House historians can be crucial to the planning process in historic preservation by participating in surveys or inventories of buildings in their areas. By doing "windshield" surveys, researchers may get a quick overview of an area. Local preservation groups or State Historic Preservation Offices often ask house historians to conduct local surveys or to prepare nominations to the National Register of Historic Places. These groups may need surveys done on a geographic (township or county) or thematic (houses by a particular architect or houses dating from a particular time) basis.

House historians may help owners with renovation or rehabilitation efforts. Before Victorian architecture became popular again in the 1970s, many people "restored" such houses by adding colonial touches to make the buildings look more "historic." As home owners rediscovered Victorian architecture, however, they became aware of more appropriate treatments.

Research into the history of a building may also generate ideas for new ways to use it. If it can no longer be a home, could it be converted to offices? In this case, the house historian will need to understand the structure of the house before construction work begins. Knowing as much as possible about the history of the building may help unravel unusual construction features that dictate whether it can be adapted to other uses.

The work of house historians is vital because preservation without interpretation is of little value in teaching history. Telling the story of a house or site can be as simple as an outdoor sign or a plaque noting the name and date of a privately owned and occupied home in a historic district, or as complicated as a multimedia production to introduce visitors to a nationally significant home. The American Association for State and Local History (AASLH) has many publications to guide house historians interested in interpretive programs for the public. Some of these are cited in the "Suggested Readings" section of this chapter.

The house historian may conduct research resulting in enough information to produce a brochure or article, to prepare a tour, or even to write a book. After conducting a neighborhood survey, the historian could develop a self-guided neighborhood tour. Walking tours and brochures can increase the neighborhood residents' enthusiasm for establishing a historic district or provide visitors with an introduction to a new area.

The historian may adapt the research for presentation in slide-tape programs and video tapes to interpret a historic site. The program could show how a house or neighborhood was restored or show visitors, including the handicapped, parts of a building that are not accessible. Such presentations could re-create a day in the lives of the residents when some prominent person visited the house. Or the presentations could illustrate everyday period tasks like cooking or cleaning in a house museum.

If there is sufficient information, the house historian may write an article for a newspaper, popular magazine, or scholarly journal, especially if the house under study reflects a trend in construction techniques, the work of a par-

---

Preservation Terms

Preservationists define the work they do in various ways. To be precise, *historic preservation* can be defined as "generally, saving from destruction or deterioration old and historic buildings, sites, structures and objects and providing for their continued use by means of restoration, rehabilitation or adaptive use." Specifically, historic preservation is "the act or process of applying measures to sustain the existing form, integrity, and material of a building or structure, and the existing form and vegetative cover of a site. It may include stabilization work, where necessary, as well as ongoing maintenance of the historic building materials," according to the *Secretary of the Interior's Standards for Rehabilitation and Guidelines for Rehabilitating Historic Buildings.*

By the Secretary's standards, *stabilization* is "the act or process of applying measures designed to reestablish a weather-resistant enclosure and the structural stability of an unsafe or deteriorated property while maintaining the essential form as it exists at present." *Preservation* is "the act or process of applying measures to sustain the existing form, integrity, and material of a building or structure, and the existing form and vegetative cover of a site. It may include initial stabilization work, where necessary, as well as ongoing maintenance of the historic building materials." *Rehabilitation* is "the act or process of returning a property to a state of utility through repair or alteration which makes possible an efficient contemporary use while preserving those portions or features of the property which are significant to its historical, architectural, and cultural values." *Reconstruction* is "the act or process of reproducing by new construction the exact form and detail of a vanished building, structure, or object, or a part thereof, as it appeared at a specific period of time." *Restoration* is "the act or process of accurately recovering the form and details of a property and its setting as it appeared at a particular period of time by means of the removal of later work or by the replacement of missing earlier work."

Since true "restoration" is the purest, and the most costly, form of work to be done on a building, such work is usually reserved for extremely important structures. Private homes are rarely restored, because to do so would require eliminating all later additions, any modern conveniences, and security systems. Few home owners are amenable to the idea of living without indoor plumbing as they would have to do if their houses were built before indoor plumbing was available. Instead, home owners want to use air-conditioning and security systems, discretely hidden to help protect the historic fabric of the building. The retention of modern conveniences turns the process of "restoration" into "preservation."

Terms like "renovation" or "rehabilitation," therefore, are more appropriate than "restoration" when discussing the work most often done on historic houses. Home owners strip woodwork, repair porches and gutters, repaint and repaper interiors. They may install modern reproductions of early-twentieth-century bathrooms and kitchens, but they do not want to have to reblack the stove every year. Good documentation and careful analysis of how the house will be used can and should lead to a happy compromise.

The *National Register of Historic Places* is a list of buildings, sites, districts, structures, and objects important in American history, archaeology, culture, or architecture. An outgrowth of the Historic Sites Act of 1935, which established the National Historic Landmarks program, the register was expanded in 1966. It is maintained through the U.S. Department of the Interior, and nominations can be made to the register by contacting the State Historic Preservation Offices. The register provides some protection to listed or eligible properties when federal funding, licensing, or permitting is involved in a project.

ticular architect, historical events, or social customs. Published architectural histories of neighborhoods, cities, or states are popular and can be commercially successful. Presentations at local, state, or national meetings can also disseminate the results of house history research.

Finally, the house historian may present his or her research findings through exhibits—permanent installations for museums, traveling exhibits, or modest displays for school projects. Exhibits could discuss such topics as a style of housing construction, architectural history throughout the state, or the work of particular builders.

Whatever the questions asked, method of presentation, purpose of research, or sources used, house historians need to recognize that the history of a building fits into a larger pattern of American life. Just as the history of an individual is shaped by broader forces in history, so too is the history of a home. House histories, then, can contribute to the public's understanding of local and social history.

Suggested Readings

House historians interested in the uses of house research will find valuable information in William T. Alderson and Shirley Payne Low, *Interpretation of Historic Sites* (Nashville: American Association for State and Local History, 1976); Jay Anderson, *Time Machines: The World of Living History* (Nashville: American Association for State and Local History, 1984); and Frederick L. Rath, Jr., and Merrilyn Rogers O'Connell, eds., *Historic Preservation: A Bibliography on Historical Organization Practices* (Nashville: American Association for State and Local History, 1975). Shirley Hanson and Nancy Hubby, *Preserving and Maintaining the Older Home* (New York: McGraw-Hill Book Company, 1983) is a comprehensive guide for owners of old houses, and Katherine Chrisman, *Dreaming in the Dust: Restoring an Old House* (Boston: Houghton Mifflin, 1986) is the two-year saga of her family's efforts to renovate a historic house. *All About Old Buildings: The Whole Preservation Catalog*, edited by Diane Maddex (Washington, D.C.: Preservation Press, 1985) is a comprehensive bibliography on historic preservation sources. Theodore J. Karamanski's "Historical Resource Management," in *The Craft of Public History: An Annotated Select Bibliography*, edited by David F. Trask and Robert W. Pomeroy, III (Westport, Conn.: Greenwood Press, 1983), provides an excellent bibliography on that specialized topic.

For assistance in compiling research materials, see Thomas E. Felt, *Researching, Writing, and Publishing Local History* (Nashville: American Association for State and Local History, 1976).

Interesting approaches to teaching children about their environment and history can be found in Gerald A. Danzer and Lawrence W. McBride, *People, Space, and Time: The Chicago Neighborhood History Project—An Introduction to Community History for Schools* (Lanham, Md.: University Press of America for Chicago Metro History Fair, Inc., 1986) and in David Weitzman, *My Backyard History Book* (Boston: Little, Brown and Company, 1975), which include children's activities in genealogy, family and neighborhood history, and photography and projects using family archives, oral history, artifacts, and buildings.

House tours, workshops, and conferences sponsored by national, state, or local organizations are opportunities to meet other house historians. Local historical or genealogical societies, historic preservation organizations, State Historic Preservation Offices, the American Association for State and Local History, the National Trust for Historic Preservation (1785 Massachusetts Avenue, N.W., Washington, D.C. 20036), and Heritage Canada Foundation (P.O. Box 1358, Station B, Ottawa, Ontario, Canada K1P 5R4) can provide information about such programs and about local resources and organizations of interest to house historians.

The definitions of preservation terms included in the sidebar to this chapter are from the *Secretary of the Interior's Standards for Rehabilitation and Guidelines for Rehabilitating Historic Buildings*, as quoted in Diane Maddex, ed., *The Brown Book: A Directory of Preservation Information* (Washington, D.C.: Preservation Press, 1983).

For information on nominating properties to the National Register, see U.S. Department of the Interior, National Park Service, Interagency Resources Division, *National Register Bulletin No. 16, Guidelines for Completing National Register of Historic Places Forms* (Washington, D.C.: Government Printing Office, 1986).

·PART I·
Searching for Clues

·2·

A Home's Setting

A HOME'S SETTING, OR LANDSCAPE, IS A FUNDAMENTAL part of its identity. "Landscape," notes historian John Stilgoe, is "a slippery word. It means more than scenery painting, a pleasant rural vista, or ornamental planting around a country house. It means shaped land, land modified for permanent human occupation, for dwelling, agriculture, manufacturing, government, worship, and for pleasure." Landscape, in Stilgoe's view, includes the neighborhood, "that space beyond their own property in which [Americans] had vital interests, close knowledge, and frequent reasons to travel."

Landscapes have both natural and human-made elements. Human-made or cultural landscapes reveal the impact of human activity on the natural landscape. Just as the natural and the cultural landscapes change over time, a building's relationship to its setting may change.

Transportation and the Landscape

Transportation routes provide a good example of the influence of natural and cultural landscapes on housing. Navigable rivers shaped initial American settlement patterns, with wharves, warehouses, and public landings placed next to them. Canals built to link rivers or to open lands for settlement spurred the growth or creation of towns along their routes. Railroads cut paths across the landscape, sometimes following the rivers but increasingly going where there was no river valley to follow. From 1850 to 1871, railroad companies encouraged commercial settlement along their routes. Speculators bought land near rights-of-way, and if the railroad bypassed a town, people sometimes moved their businesses or homes to new locations by the tracks.

9

Early roads, as well, often followed river valleys. Along roads such as the National Road (now U.S. 40), houses frequently were set quite close to the thoroughfare, and taverns and stores clustered around crossroads. Roads evolved without an overall plan in many eastern and southern rural areas. As the nation grew and the automobile became the dominant mode of transportation, residential, industrial, and retail centers sprang up in undeveloped farmland.

The 1956 Federal Highway Act authorized the development of a nationwide interstate highway system that poured a swath of concrete pavement across the nation. Super highways, tearing through the heart of most major cities, destroyed housing and cut off neighborhoods. At the same time, the highways promoted rapid growth near highway exits.

Some suburban communities organized around airparks, marinas, country clubs, or golf courses. Beginning in the mid-1950s, housing developments as widely separated as Lake Geneva Aire Estates at Lake Geneva, Wisconsin, and Eagles Landing at Williamson, Georgia, were established around airstrips. Residents, it was assumed, would have small private planes; neighborhood restrictions could require, as did those in Spruce Creek near Daytona Beach, Florida, that "hangars match the architectural style of the homes they accompany." The 1960's "new towns" of Columbia, Maryland, and Reston, Virginia, featured lakes with marina facilities, so that residents could row their boats from home to the community shopping center. Elsewhere, housing clustered around golf courses provided easy access to the residents' favorite sport. Although not common, these communities reflect the diversity of housing choices available to Americans.

Landscape Features

Researchers can learn much about rural landscape features. One can examine a farm's fields, crops, and buildings; routes used to move through the area; the location of trees and shrubs for functional or ornamental purposes; natural features, including rivers, prairies, mountains, and soil conditions; boundary demarcations, such as fences, walls, and hedgerows; the type, function, materials, and construction of structures, including buildings, cemeteries, dams, canals, and bridges; small-scale elements, like cattle chutes, water troughs, or isolated grave markers; and finally, perceptual qualities, such as smells and sounds.

The settlement patterns, demography, and archaeological remains of a rural area reflect its historical and cultural context. The apparently out-of-scale

The photograph of this isolated Montana wheat ranch shows about 200 of the 320 acres received by Jesse Grimes under the Homestead Act of 1909. The initial breaking of the sod into productive soil, and the 1930's development of strip farming, changed the face of the landscape. Many homesteads were located along roads near the horizon seen on this photograph, but crop failures drove some families away. Now most roads have been plowed under, but old maps and land records might identify their precise locations.

Roman Catholic churches in rural west-central Ohio, for example, mirror the overwhelming German Catholic presence in the area and the influence of a particularly forceful priest. House historians in that area should consider the residents' relationship to the church.

Cultural Boundaries

Even the study of a modern suburban neighborhood may answer questions about a formerly rural landscape. Is an original farmhouse anywhere to be seen? Has a stream been channelled into a sewer pipe? Do any of the subdivision's roads follow remnants of farm lanes? Elimination of all vestiges of a farm is in itself significant; the area was probably developed all at once instead of by a farmer selling off a lot or two at a time.

Additional pointers for examining the urban landscape (or cityscape) are discussed in Grady Clay's *Close-Up: How to Read the American City.* Clay suggests looking for a space that defines the center of the community, such as a public square or village green, and for street pattern irregularities that may show surveying errors or grids planned by different developers.

In urban areas, houses often gain their architectural or historical significance by being part of a larger neighborhood landscape that evokes a distinctive sense of time and place. Recognized historic districts may be marked by boundary signs or plaques on the houses or shown on tour brochures. Some city districts, such as Vieux Carre in New Orleans, Old Town in Alexandria, Virginia, and Beacon Hill in Boston, are heavily guarded by zoning, historic district legislation, and National Register of Historic Places status. Other historic districts may be protected simply by owners striving to keep the neighborhood intact and special. The entire town of Silverton, Colorado, for example, is listed on the National Register but has no other protective legislation.

Some neighborhoods are set off by physical or geographic barriers. Private streets, such as Munger Place in Dallas, Texas, were designed with gates to give a visible sign that the residents wished to be isolated from the rest of the city. Housing for managers of the Anaconda Copper Mining Company's Refinery, Zinc Plant, and Wiremill in Black Eagle, Montana, sat on a hill inside a compound surrounded by gates that were monitored by a company guard. Single-entrance apartment buildings with human or electronic "gatekeepers" are modern equivalents that offer residents physical protection and social status.

Examining the boundaries of the city is also instructive. Strip development along major arteries or the "fast food exits" on the interstate system may obscure surviving farmhouses. Houses converted to commercial spaces may remain relatively intact or be engulfed by commercial additions.

The Role of Governments

For four centuries, governmental decisions at all levels have played a role in American housing. Governments took initiatives in colonial America to ensure easily defended town sites, an adequate, safe water supply, and space for agriculture, housing, and public buildings—initiatives that had an impact on the towns' physical layouts. The earliest example of such governmental action came in 1573 when the Spanish government began to control the town plans for its pueblos or civil towns through King Philip II's Laws of the Indies. Enforced during the Spanish colonial occupation of the Americas, the codes dictated the general town layout, location of key buildings and house sites, construction standards, and other details to guarantee a successful settlement.

The English, who began planning New World communities with the founding of Jamestown in 1607, and the French were not as restrictive as the Spanish, but French and English colonial governments did dictate some community plans. These may be seen today in the very different street layouts of New Orleans and Quebec, Williamsburg and Annapolis, Philadelphia and Savannah.

New England towns reflected the several different land use systems that then prevailed in England, including the use of common lands. While common farmlands did not endure, farmers long shared common clay pits and meadows. These New England towns contrasted sharply with the isolated homes built on large, individually owned land-grant parcels in the South.

After the Revolutionary War, government planning continued to influence the urban cultural landscape. For example, the 1811 redesign for the City of New York divided the city into twenty-five-by-one-hundred-foot lots, a process that encouraged real estate speculation and imprinted on the island of Manhattan a grid pattern that plagued housing reformers later in the century. The high value of these rectangular lots encouraged developers to erect buildings in which they could rent space to as many people as possible. The dense construction cut off light and air to most of the city's inhabitants.

Farther west, the Public Land Act of 1785, incorporated into the Northwest Ordinance of 1787, determined the landscape of rural America north and west of the Ohio River, land known as the Northwest Territory. The ordinance determined how states would be created from this tract of land and controlled settlement patterns by deciding, before land was sold, how it would be surveyed. There, large farms on straight north-south and east-west roads contrasted with the tightly clustered towns along river valleys in the New England and Middle Atlantic states.

Settlers moved west to claim land for farming, ranching, and mining throughout the nineteenth century, and they built farmsteads, cattle towns, and mining communities as they went. Across the Great Plains, settlers and speculators took advantage of the Homestead Act of 1862 to claim free 160-acre rectangular plats of land surveyed under the Public Land Act. As they fenced off their land with inexpensive barbed wire, patented in 1874, grain farming replaced cattle driving as a major economic activity from the Mississippi River to the Rocky Mountains.

Interest in city planning intensified because of the Chicago 1893 Colum-bian Exposition, Ebenezeer Howard's garden city movement, and efforts by early-twentieth-century urban reformers to provide a healthy environment. The Columbian Exposition promoted the concept of "city beautiful" plan-ning, concentrating on large governmental and cultural buildings. Garden city advocates looked for ways to combine green space, good housing, indus-trial sites, and commercial buildings. These efforts were part of the general concern in the Progressive era with beautifying cities and solving society's problems through governmental action and private philanthropy.

The federal government molded the cultural landscape by creating about a hundred new communities in formerly rural areas during the 1930s. Unlike older cities that grew organically over time, these communities were planned from the beginning to serve a governmental purpose—to provide a fresh start in life for qualified residents who were selected on the basis of income and their ability and willingness to participate in these experimental communities.

Franklin D. Roosevelt's administration initiated three well-known green-belt towns, Greendale, Wisconsin; Greenhills, Ohio; and Greenbelt, Mary-land. Each greenbelt town was protected by a band of green space encircling it. Remnants of these belts are still visible and are protected, at least in Greenhills, Ohio, by strict zoning regulations prohibiting development in the belt.

Recording Landscape Features

Why explore the influence of the landscape on a house? For one thing, a historic district nomination for the National Register of Historic Places must include some justification of the district's boundaries. Natural features, such as creeks or hills, may distinguish the district from its surroundings. Or government policy, such as the establishment of a greenbelt or the con-struction of a highway, may separate the district from its neighbors. Record-ing the current landscape may help the historian determine whether the historical character of the district is still intact.

Documenting the landscape is crucial if owners are interested in protect-ing their property by donating a scenic easement to a preservation or con-servation group. Scenic easements are legal tools that protect the landscape around a building. While scenic easements are used primarily in rural areas, facade easements to protect the exterior of the structure can be important in both rural and urban areas. Both kinds of easements can be used separately or together.

There are several techniques to record or document the landscape. Paper, pen, tape recorder, and camera are useful tools in such work. A good way to begin the recording process is to prepare a sketch map showing the location of the building in relation to streets or roads. If the home is in a row of houses in an urban neighborhood, note how many are in the row, whether there are small yards or walks between pairs of houses sharing common walls, where alleys cut through the block, and where buildings have been demolished. If the houses in the neighborhood are detached, note any particularly large lots; a house that previously occupied the site may have been demolished, or for some reason, a building may never have been built there. Use a tape measure to get the dimensions of the structure and its distance from the street and the nearby intersections. If the house is in a rural area, you may need to measure the distance to an intersection or local landmark by noting the mileage on a car or bicycle odometer. These measurements will later be invaluable in interpreting maps, photographs, and legal records.

Also show on the map any distinguishing features—both natural and human-made—on the landscape: garages, carriage houses, barns, outhouses, driveways, old trees or hedges, gardens, fence lines, and streams. Rough measurements of distances between buildings and other features will be useful. Also note trees that are significantly older than others in the area, hedgerows or stone fences that may indicate old property lines, and curious "leftover" outbuildings or foundations. Much can be learned from these seemingly stray facts. For example, two of the authors have houses on lots carved from the same farm. The former owner of the farm, a railroad freight agent, planted unclaimed saplings, which grew into an orchard of fruit trees. After the farm was subdivided and houses were built in the area in the 1960s, some of the trees planted by the farm's former owner remained.

The names of neighborhoods or landscape features that you include on your map may refer to individuals, ethnic groups, or geographic features that can provide clues to the area's history. For example, San Francisco's Chinatown suggests the community's distinctive ethnic origin, which helps explain the architecture of some of its oldest buildings and the names of its streets and businesses. Clues about other neighborhood names may be harder to unravel but may recall the name of an early landowner. The historian can later check these names in library sources or public records.

While making a map, it is useful to photograph the house under study and its environment to compare current and historical photographs and to supplement research notes. Aerial photos, topographical maps from various

Historians can learn significant facts by surveying stylistic variations in a given area. More than 200 similar houses were identified between Guelph and Meldrum Bay, Ontario. Many on the mainland were brick (middle). Most Manitoulin Island examples were frame (upper left); a few were faced with stone or "modernized" as Classical Revival by applying a stucco veneer and adding trim (upper right and lower left). An oral history interview of the owner of the house at Gore Bay (lower right) confirmed that the facade was "drawn from" the traditional style and that all bricks had to be imported to the island. The house at upper right also reveals traditional roofing techniques.

dates, and old atlases help the historian trace changes in the location of outbuildings, woodlots, hedgerows, windbreak trees, fence rows, roads, ponds, and other elements of the natural landscape. Long-abandoned fields and fence rows may appear on infrared photographs or may be found by trekking through the woods, particularly in New England and the South, where farms were abandoned when the owners moved to towns or as they planted in new areas when the soil wore out.

Next, take a careful look around the building. Whatever the type of home, the basic examination techniques are the same: look, touch, smell, and listen. Have new buildings been built among the old in the neighborhood? The presence of new buildings might indicate a redirection of the neighborhood; a lack of them, efforts to perpetuate the existing economic mix. How well do new buildings blend with the old? Have most of the buildings been altered in a similar fashion? Are all the houses well maintained, perhaps indicating a stable neighborhood of owner-occupied housing? Are many houses for sale or for rent, indicating a transient neighborhood or one undergoing economic decline or rampant rehabilitation? Does the community being examined give evidence of cottage industries as Lynn, Massachusetts, does with its backyard shoemakers' cottages?

Houses erected before or after most of the others in a neighborhood will often be conspicuous and out of scale. Owners of an old farmhouse or suburban mansion that once sat in the middle of a large lot may have sold all the surrounding land for subdivision plots. An isolated grand country house overlooking a junkyard clearly attests to changing land use. If all the houses in the neighborhood look roughly the same, sit on the same size lots, and are the same distance from the street, restrictions or zoning codes were likely in force when the houses were built.

Consider how the design of a house is affected by the surrounding topography. In hilly areas, a house with two stories above grade on the street side may be five stories in the back. Builders in cities such as Wilmington, Delaware, and San Francisco, California, stepped rowhouses up hillsides to accommodate the terrain.

An alert observer may learn much about the life styles of the neighborhood residents. What smells and sounds are noticeable? Spices from ethnic cooking in the halls of an apartment complex? The distinctive odors from a factory? Country or classical music? One of the authors lived in a neighborhood in Philadelphia where it was possible on a summer night to hear Latin rhythm music from street musicians blending with classical music from the stereos of new residents who were renovating some houses in the area. Are there swing sets in the yards, showing that the neighborhood has many children living there, or is everyone middle-aged or elderly? Does the neighborhood appear to be racially mixed or homogeneous? Are signs in a foreign language as well as in English, indicating a strong ethnic influence in the neighborhood? Do people congregate in back yards, or do they prefer to lounge on front steps or converse through windows to friends in the street? Do people have access from the street to backyards?

It is useful to note the economic and social activity in the area. Is it a mixed residential-commercial neighborhood, with some houses converted to stores? What services does the neighborhood offer? Where do residents shop? Do nearby stores provide most of the services residents need on a daily basis? Are there traditional neighborhood groceries, or does every grocery sell white wine, brie, and the *New York Times*? Have used furniture stores become antique stores? Have ten-cent stores been converted into pottery shops, indicating a neighborhood whose residents go elsewhere for toothpaste and food? Do art galleries and pawn shops sit side by side, suggesting an area in transition?

What religious denominations are common? Are any religious buildings, such as conservative Jewish synagogues or Greek Orthodox churches, identified with particular ethnic groups? Have the churches clearly changed denominations? What might be concluded if the building's cornerstone says "Presbyterian," but the current sign says "Apostolic"? In an Amish or Mennonite neighborhood, one might note the absence of electric lines, television antennas, and satellite dishes.

In a rural area, is the feed store still open to serve farmers? Are the grain elevators operational? Is the traditional small-town school still serving as the center of community life, or has new housing been built around a modern consolidated school? Is the post office still functioning as a center of community identity? Are old barns and sheds actively used for machinery and animals? Are fields still farmed? What crops are grown? Do farms look prosperous? Are the outhouses and pumps still in use? Are there smoke houses or summer kitchens? Slave quarters now converted to apartments? Carriage houses or stables? Are the gardens abandoned, and the walls collapsing?

After examining the landscape, the house historian will be in a better position to turn to the particular building being studied. Photographs, maps, and sketches gathered during this early research stage will, in turn, become part of the house's history.

Suggested Readings

Many of the standard reference works that one might use in researching a house history deal with several topics. Because so many of the sources on landscapes and building exteriors are interrelated, their bibliographies are combined here. Additional sources on vernacular, folk, or regional housing can be found in chapter 7. A librarian can help in a search for the materials cited in this book as well as in a search for special collections, indexes, or computerized materials available to aid researchers.

For general information on landscapes, see Robert Z. Melnick, *Rural Historic Districts in the National Park Service* (Washington, D.C.: U.S. Department of the Interior, 1984) and John Stilgoe, *Common Landscape of America, 1580 to 1845* (New Haven: Yale University Press, 1982). Stilgoe's book has an excellent bibliography and includes sections on the impor-tance of roads as internal improvements, a brief introduction to the history of city plan-ning, and information on the public land survey (the quotation in this chapter is from page 12). Grady Clay's *Close-Up: How to Read the American City* (Chicago: University of Chicago Press, 1973 and 1980) provides clues on understanding the "cityscape." A handy and easy-to-use manual for studying American history by examining its landscape features and buildings is Douglass L. Brownstone's *A Field Guide to American History* (New York: Facts on File, Inc., 1984), which covers everything from soil to wallpaper and includes an architectural glossary and short bibliography. *Clues to American Gardens*, by David P. Fogle and Catherine Mahan (Washington, D.C.: Starrhill Press, 1986), is a handy field guide for examining colonial gardens to mail-order Sears, Roebuck and Co. gardens and con-tainer gardens. For those interested in preserving landscapes, Rudy J. Favretti and Joy Put-nam Favretti's *Landscapes and Gardens for Historic Buildings: A Handbook for Reproducing and Creating Authentic Landscape Settings* (Nashville: American Association for State and Local History, 1979) is an important resource. Additional references on geographic and eco-logical relationships may be found in Thomas Schlereth's "Historic Houses as Learning Laboratories: Seven Teaching Strategies," American Association for State and Local His-tory Technical Leaflet 105, *History News* 33:4 (April 1978).

Some ideas in this chapter came from John W. Reps, *Town Planning In Frontier America* (Princeton: Princeton University Press, 1969) and "Home is Where the Hangar Is," *Airline Pilot* 53 (December 1984): 8-15ff.

There are a number of standard bibliographies available, including those in David E. Kyvig and Myron A. Marty, *Nearby History: Exploring the Past around You* (Nashville: Ameri-can Association for State and Local History, 1982); the bibliography for the "Landscapes and Buildings" chapter is especially useful. Other bibliographies include the National Trust for Historic Preservation's *All About Old Buildings: The Whole Preservation Catalog*, edited by Diane Maddex (Washington, D.C.: Preservation Press, 1985); James C. Massey's *Read-ings in Historic Preservation* (Washington, D.C.: National Preservation Institute, 1986); the *Catalog of the Avery Memorial Architectural Library, Columbia University*, 2nd ed., enlarged, 5th supplement, 4 vols. (Boston: G. K. Hall & Co., 1982); Bernard Kapel's *Arts in America: A Bibliography*, 4 vols. (Washington, D.C.: Smithsonian Institution Press, 1979); *The Historic Preservation Yearbook: A Documentary Record of Significant Policy Developments and Issues*, edited by Russell V. Keune (Bethesda, Md.: Adler & Adler, Publishers, Inc., in coopera-tion with the National Trust for Historic Preservation, 1985); and Henry-Russell Hitchcock's *American Architectural Books: A List of Books, Portfolios, and Pamphlets on Architecture and Related Subjects Published in America before 1895,* 1946 (Minneapolis: University of Minnesota Press, 1962).

Periodicals can be located through *Art Index; The Architectural Index; Avery Index to Architectural Periodicals;* and *Art and Archaeology Technical Abstracts.* This last publication, formerly titled *ITC Abstracts,* is useful because it indexes *APT Bulletin; American Paintings and Coatings Journal; History News;* and similar journals. The other indexes mentioned cover *Historic Preservation; Interior Design; Interiors; Architectural Digest; Journal of the Society of Architectural Historians; Landscape Architecture;* and *Ninteenth Century.*

Other relevant periodicals include: *Agora; American Heritage; Americana; Architectural Record; American Architect; Architect; Architecture: The AIA Journal; Inland Architect; JAPA: Journal of the American Planning Association; Journal of Garden History; Journal of Housing; Living Historical Farms Bulletin; The Old-House Journal; Places: A Quarterly Journal of Environmental Design; Planning; Progressive Architecture; Real Estate Finance; SITES; Small Town;* and *Town & Country.*

More specialized journals can also be useful. These include those focused on a particular time period like *Colonial Williamsburg* and *Yankee;* regional architecture magazines like *Architecture Minnesota* or *Metropolis: The Architecture & Design Magazine of New York;* periodicals aimed at particular building styles, such as *The Brownstoner,* the newsletter of the Brownstone Revival Committee in New York City; folk journals such as *The Clarion* or *Early American Life;* and those focused on the decorative arts, such as *The Decorative Arts Trust Newsletter. Arizona Highways* and similar publications provide information on how the landscape affects a house's history.

Publications issued by local or statewide history or historic preservation organizations provide up-to-date information on sources in the state. Check with your state's major historical society for a list of publications in your area.

To learn more about architects, consult Diane Maddex, ed., *Master Builders: A Guide to Famous American Architects* (Washington, D.C.: Preservation Press, 1985); Adolf Placzek, *Macmillan Encyclopedia of Architects,* 4 vols. (New York: The Free Press, 1982); J. M. Richards, ed., *Who's Who in Architecture from 1400 to the Present* (New York: Holt, Rinehart and Winston, 1977); Henry W. Schirmer, *Profile: The Official Directory of Architectural Firms* (Philadelphia: Archimedia, 1980); and Henry F. Withey and Elsie Rathburn Withey, *Biographical Dictionary of American Architects (Deceased),* 1956 (Los Angeles: Hennessey & Ingalls, Inc., 1970). Landscape architecture firms may be identified through the American Society of Landscape Architects Professional Practice Institute's *1984-85 National Directory of Landscape Architectural Firms* (Washington, D.C.: American Society of Landscape Architects, 1984).

Those interested in housing colors should consult Roger Moss's *Century of Color: Exterior Decoration for American Buildings, 1820-1920* (Watkins Glen, N.Y.: The American Life Foundation, 1981).

Basic introductions to architectural history and building technology include John J-G. Blumenson, *Identifying American Architecture: A Pictorial Guide to Styles and Terms, 1600-1945* (Nashville: American Association for State and Local History, 1981); John C. Poppelier, S. Allen Chambers, Jr., and Nancy B. Schwartz, *What Style Is It? A Guide to American Architecture* (Washington, D.C.: Preservation Press, 1983); and Marilyn W. Klein and David

P. Fogle, *Clues to American Architecture*, rev. ed. (Washington, D.C.: Starrhill Press, 1986). These are available in a format that is easy to carry while working in the field.

The *American House* by Mary Mix Foley (New York: Harper & Row, 1980) provides an architectural history focused only on housing and discusses European traditions for American housing and variations of styles. Broader surveys of architectural history include Marcus Whiffen and Frederick Koeper, *American Architecture*, 2 vols. (Cambridge, Mass.: The MIT Press, 1981) and David P. Handlin, *American Architecture* (London: Thames & Hudson, 1985). Carole Rifkind's *A Field Guide to American Architecture* (New York: New American Library, 1980) uses measured drawings and occasional photographs to illustrate American architectural styles. Virginia and Lee McAlester's *A Field Guide to American Houses* (New York: A. A. Knopf, 1984) should also be a standard reference source. For vernacular architecture, consult the "Suggested Readings" in chapter 7.

There are many specialized studies of particular regions, architects, types of housing, and time periods, including Thomas Aidala, *The Great Houses of San Francisco* (New York: A. A. Knopf, 1981); Robert Gamble, *The Alabama Catalog: Historic American Buildings Survey, A Guide to the Early Architecture of the State* (Tuscaloosa, Ala.: The University of Alabama Press, 1986); Fiske Kimball, *Domestic Architecture of the American Colonies and of the Early Republic, 1922* (New York: Dover Publications, 1966); William J. Murtagh, "The Philadelphia Row House," in *Journal of the Society of Architectural Historians* 14 (December 1957); Henry-Russell Hitchcock, *The Architecture of H. H. Richardson and His Times* (Cambridge: The MIT Press, 1966); Peg Sinclair and Taylor Lewis, *Victorious Victorians: A Guide to the Major Architectural Styles* (New York: Holt, Reinhart & Winston, 1985); Randolph DeLahanty and Andrew E. McKinney, *Preserving the West* (New York: Pantheon Books, 1985); and Clay Lancaster, *The American Bungalow, 1880-1930* (New York: Abbeville Press, 1985). Carrol Van West's *A Traveler's Companion to Montana History* (Helena: Montana Historical Society Press, 1986) is an excellent example of a travel guide that links the landscape and buildings to the lives of the residents. J. Randall Cotton has written a two-part series on "The Great American Garage" in *The Old-House Journal* (September 1986, pp. 328-335; October 1986, pp. 382-390) to help house historians analyze this most ubiquitous twentieth-century outbuilding.

Major historical architecture surveys include Frances Benjamin Johnston's *The Carnegie Survey of the Architecture of the South*, published on microfiche from the collection in the Prints and Photographs Division of the Library of Congress; the microfiche edition of *The Historic American Buildings Survey*, with separate editions for each state; and a microfiche edition of eight volumes of C. W. Short and R. Stanley-Brown's *Survey of the Architecture of Completed Projects of the Public Works Administration* (U.S. Committee on Architectural Surveys). All three surveys have been prepared in microfiche by Chadwick-Healey, Inc. (623 Martense Avenue, Teaneck, New Jersey 07666).

Architectural dictionaries and encyclopedias often assume that the researcher has a knowledge of architectural history or construction techniques. Basic sources in this category include John Fleming, Hugh Honour, and Nikolaus Pevsner, *The Penguin Dictionary of Architecture* (Harmondsworth, Middlesex, England: Penguin Books, 1966); John S. Scott, *The Penguin Dictionary of Building*, 2nd ed. (Harmondsworth, Middlesex, England: Penguin Books, 1974); Henry H. Saylor, *Dictionary of Architecture* (New York: John Wiley & Sons, 1952); Cyril M. Harris, ed., *Historic Architecture Sourcebook* (New York: McGraw-Hill Book Co., 1977);

and William Dudley Hunt, Jr., *Encyclopedia of American Architecture* (New York: McGraw-Hill Book Co., 1980). The *Housing/Planning Glossary* by Harold B. Olin and Christina B. Farnsworth was published in 1979 by the United States League of Savings Associations to provide a glossary of housing, planning, and lending terms; this is for sale by the United States League of Savings Institutions (formerly the USLSA), 111 East Wacker Drive, Chicago, Illinois 60601.

If a house or neighborhood is listed on the National Register of Historic Places, it may be possible to get a copy of the nomination form from your State Historic Preservation Officer or a local preservation organization. Unfortunately, there is no one publication that contains all entries on the National Register, but the following sources may be consulted: U.S. Department of the Interior, National Park Service, *The National Register of Historic Places* (Washington, D.C.: Government Printing Office, 1976), which includes all properties listed through December 31, 1974, by state and county; and U.S. Department of the Interior, Heritage Conservation and Recreation Service, *The National Register of Historic Places*, vol. 2 (Washington, D.C.: Government Printing Office, n.d.), including all listings from January 1, 1975, to December 31, 1976. There has been no subsequent comprehensive publication of the register, but each February or March, the U.S. Department of the Interior publishes in the *Federal Register* a listing of those properties entered during the previous calendar year. A microfiche edition of National Register listings through 1982 has been published by Chadwick-Healey, Inc.; the edition includes reproductions of photographs and texts for nominations and is available on a state-by-state basis.

Several books on material culture by Thomas Schlereth may be useful to house historians interested in furnishings or the landscape: *Artifacts and the American Past* (Nashville: American Association for State and Local History, 1980), *Material Culture Studies in America* (Nashville: American Association for State and Local History, 1982), and *Material Culture: A Research Guide* (Lawrence: University Press of Kansas, 1985). See also the bibliography on artifacts in Kyvig and Marty's *Nearby History*, pp. 161-164.

Alan Gowan's *Images of American Living: Four Centuries of Architecture and Furniture as Cultural Expression* (New York: Harper & Row, 1964) and Robert Bishop and Patricia Coblentz's *The World of Antiques, Art, and Architecture in Victorian America* (New York: E. P. Dutton, 1979) are useful for house historians because of their emphasis on furniture design.

Useful works on geography and land-use development include: Terry G. Jordan and Lester Rowntree, *The Human Mosaic: A Thematic Introduction to Cultural Geography*, 4th ed. (New York: Harper & Row, 1986); Ralph H. Brown, *Historical Geography of the United States* (New York: Harcourt, Brace, & World, Inc., 1948), which includes an overview of the development of the United States from the colonial period to 1870; F. J. Marschner, *Land Use and Its Patterns in the United States*, Agricultural Handbook No. 153 (Washington, D.C.: Government Printing Office, 1959), which contains a collection of aerial photos demonstrating settlement patterns in the United States; Hildegard Binder Johnson, *Order Upon the Land: The U.S. Rectangular Land Survey and the Upper Mississippi Country* (New York: Oxford University Press, 1976), a study of the impact of the rectangular survey system on the landscape of the Midwest; and Norman J. Thrower, *Original Survey and Land Subdivision: A Comparative Study of the Form and Effect of Contrasting Cadastral Surveys* (Chicago: Rand McNally for the Association of American Geographers, 1966).

·3·

The Home Itself

TO READ THE EXTERIOR AND INTERIOR OF A BUILDING, the house historian follows the same principles used to read the landscape. Careful examination of the facade can provide vast amounts of information. Clues found in the interior of the building and in printed and illustrative sources may prompt the historian to return for another, even closer, look at the exterior.

The Exterior of the Home

It is a good idea first to identify the house's precise location. Look for an address on the mailbox or street curb or the name of a building on a cornerstone or datestone. A house may have two addresses, an old one set in the stained glass transom over the door or carved into the door lintel and a new one on the mailbox. A corner house in an urban neighborhood may also have a street name on a plate bolted to one of its walls.

Before setting foot on the property, the house historian should obtain permission from the owner or occupant. If the research is part of a survey for an organization, it helps in gaining permission to carry a letter of introduction or to tell the local police or sheriff that someone will be "poking" around the neighborhood.

If the house being studied is partially obscured by heavy vegetation, the researcher may want to take equipment to clear a path. Be sure, of course, to obtain the owner's permission to cut vines or shrubs. Before exploring around foundations or under porches, check for animals living there. If the building is at all unstable or dilapidated, wear a hard hat and sturdy shoes and do not go alone.

Take a careful look at the building itself. Is it a single-family house that has been converted to apartments? Structures that once housed large families and servants often were too large or became too expensive to maintain for later residents, so the buildings were converted into apartments. Is the structure worker housing provided by a factory or mine owner for employees and located near the plant or mine shaft? In some communities, a company may once have owned all the houses, which may have been identical in construction. Over the years, as the company sold the houses, new owners may have broken the sameness with alterations such as aluminum siding and modern porches.

It helps to draw rough sketches of the site plan and elevations of the house and then note changes to the structure on these sketches. If possible, measure the length and width of the building. Look for alterations, such as porches with wrought iron pillars where wood ones were originally, or porches that have been removed totally, leaving a "scar" on the building, and note these changes on the sketches. Wood porches may have been replaced with ultra-modern designs of aluminum and glass or with careful replications almost indistinguishable from the originals.

Finding evidence of additions to the house, or deletions from it, involves looking carefully at wall surfaces. Variations in wood siding, breaks in the foundations of brick and stone walls, changes in the color or type of brick or stone, changes in the color and texture of the mortar used on brick and stone walls, and vertical lines or scars on exterior walls indicate additions or remodelings. Frustrating the house historian's attempts to locate additions or deletions are wall coverings added after the structure was built—metal siding, stucco, Fibercoat,® Insulbrick,® and shingle siding. If you determine that some type of siding has been added, take a close look at the foundations. Siding rarely hides breaks in the foundations. Siding or stucco can cover evidence of earlier window and door lintels or porches removed before the exterior skin was applied. If any siding or Insulbrick® is loose, peek underneath to see the original wall surface. Take note of the siding. Is it wood or metal? Some metal siding has been grained to look like wood and may be the size of wood clapboards, but it can be easily distinguished from wood by dents found in its surface or by the metal sound produced when it is tapped. Look for scars or stains on the walls. Cast iron used for lintels on windows and doors may have been covered with another material or porches may have been removed, but the ironwork may be detected by tell-tale rust marks down the side of the building if the metalwork was not well maintained.

Foundations may be of stone, brick, concrete block, or artificial stone (concrete block cast to look like stone). If all the units are uniform in size and texture, and the building dates from the early twentieth century, artificial stone blocks are a good possibility. These blocks may have been used as porch pillars or as replacements for stone and brick building elements for exterior walls. Sometimes metal was pressed to look like stone and used for siding or to cover a rubble stone or brick foundation.

Windows can also provide clues to changes. Original windows and doors replaced with smaller ones or extra openings cut in a wall may give an "off-balance" appearance to the facade. Single-lite sashes (one sheet of glass) may have replaced multilite, smaller pane sashes. Painted metal sashes with snap-on mullions (divisions between panes of glass) sometimes have been used to replace the original wood. When searching for former door openings, look for worn sill beams or stones that marked the entrance to the building; large stones scattered about the exterior may indicate where a stoop was located.

If the building has been painted, poke around window frames, under the eaves, around the brackets, and in other hidden spots to detect evidence of old paint schemes. Whitewashing was a common treatment for wood frame or log walls because it helped kill insects and discourage mildew. Evidence of this treatment can be found in hidden places on the walls or under vines that have grown up over the years.

Examining the roof of the building is also important in determining the house's history. The roof may be metal, tile, slate, shingle (asphalt or wood), roofing paper, or wood. If slate, the roof may well be original to a late-nineteenth-century house. Asphalt shingles designed to look like slate may be hard to detect from a distance.

Modern conveniences can also be used to date buildings or alterations to them. Attached garages were not common on houses built before the 1920s but proliferated as part of the post-World War II building boom when more people could afford cars and moved to suburbs where there was room to build garages or carports. Solar panels on houses date modifications or new construction, in most cases, to the 1970s or later.

After examining the building and its neighborhood, the researcher will be tempted to assign a style to the building. Not all buildings can be identified as high-style or academic architecture, buildings designed by an architect and in the vanguard of architectural taste. However, many buildings have high-style details, which will provide rough clues to the age of the structures. A number of guides to assist in identifying high-style buildings are listed in the bibliography of chapter 2.

After examining the exterior of the house, house historians can use some of the same techniques to look for changes on the interior. Some changes, such as alterations in the placement of windows and doors, affect the appearance of the building on both the exterior and the interior.

Friendship Hill

Friendship Hill was the home of Albert Gallatin, Secretary of the Treasury under Presidents Jefferson and Madison and Ambassador to France under President Monroe. Located in southwestern Pennsylvania near Point Marion, Friendship Hill was built on a high bluff along the Monongahela River over a period of more than 100 years. During the 1960s and 1970s, the house deteriorated, but in 1979, the National Park Service took possession of it and its 661 acres and began long-range planning for restoration and interpretation.

Friendship Hill National Historic Site, protected by the National Register of Historic Places and the National Historic Landmarks program, conveys the story of Albert Gallatin and Jeffersonian America. It gives house historians and preservationists an opportunity to examine how a house was constructed and grew over several generations of different families. In its pre-restoration condition, one can observe at least five phases of growth. Studying the house has been likened to a vertical archaeological dig: as researchers discover more evidence, they find clues to earlier styles, construction techniques, materials, and life styles.

Gallatin's letters indicate that in 1789 he built a brick house and, ten years later, constructed another section of heavy hewn timber framing and brick nogging covered with clapboard siding. From 1823 to 1824, the Gallatins added a large stone addition and a stone kitchen. Later, other owners added to the house, giving it the lopsided, sprawling appearance of a folk-vernacular style building. Throughout the life of the house, there have been attempts to make it appear more refined, uniform, and harmonious. Pencilled brick; eighteenth-, nineteenth-, and

Mr. Gallatin's Mansion.

The earliest extant illustration of Friendship Hill, near Point Marion, Pennsylvania, is a woodcut by Sherman Day, circa 1841. It aids historians in recognizing changes that have occurred and in interpreting the Gallatins's letters about the house.

twentieth-century stucco, sometimes scored and pencilled to resemble stone; partially stuccoed stone; false seaming; and connected porches and passageways are only a few of the clues to the evolution of the house's exterior.

The interior is equally intriguing and puzzling. Much of the early construction evidence—early handsplit lath and cut nails, plaster with coarse sand and animal hair, wide-board flooring, whitewashed beaded siding, windows and doors, and even scraps of wallpaper—lies beneath materials and embellishments added later. There will always be questions about which owners did what, when, and why, and, like other research, there is always the possibility of uncovering new information to add to the story.

Historians of pre-twentieth-century and rural houses often face a lack of written documentation. In the case of Friendship Hill, one would expect a wealth of material because every owner was the sort of person whose records could end up in archives—reasonably well off financially and prominent either nationally or locally. Yet, there is little information about the construction of the house and the furnishings, especially during the eighteenth and nineteenth centuries. Gallatin left thousands of letters and other documents, but most were governmental and political papers. While several hundred personal letters exist, many of which pertain to the building of his house, there is a reference to a letter that contains the major plans for his last and largest addition. That letter, unfortunately, has been lost.

Historians attempting to determine how the Gallatins furnished the house have scant information. Gallatin's letters indicate what he wanted made or purchased for his house, but few specify what was in it. Family letters give clues about the Gallatins's life style, but seldom mention material possessions. Research is complicated further because subsequent wealthy owners, knowing they were living in a famous man's home, acquired furniture that they assumed he might have had and interpreted post-Gallatin portions of the house as his. A large dining room, for instance, was added about 1895 and was known as "The State Dining Room."

The National Park Service uncovered significant clues in sources that historians of smaller houses can use. From tax records, researchers learned that in 1798 Gallatin's house was a two-story brick structure with dimensions of twenty-six-by-twenty-nine feet; the second story had seven windows with fifteen lites (panes) each; and the first story had nine windows with twelve lites each. Searching for missing windows, architectural historians uncovered them enclosed in a wall of an adjacent wing added after Gallatin sold the house.

In the Gallatin papers, available on microfilm, historians found Gallatin's description of the house in 1823 when he returned from Paris. Then, from a Pennsylvania history book published in the mid-nineteenth century, researchers found a sketch of the house, circa 1841, providing a visual document of Gallatin's written description. From photographs collected from residents of the Friendship Hill area, historians were able to document subsequent changes in porches, windows, and wings. Damage caused by fires in the 1970s exposed eighteenth- to twentieth-century construction materials and methods, further adding to the knowledge of the evolution of the house.

Visitors to Albert Gallatin's estate at Friendship Hill National Historic Site are treated to a lawn concert sponsored by the Friendship Hill Association, an organization formed to promote interest in the property. Note the addition and changes to the porch.

Family correspondence gives the National Park Service a unique opportunity to provide visitors to the site with a rich interpretation of the life of a distinguished family on the frontier. Letters describe, among other things, the Gallatins's loving relationship with and care of their children and black servants, management of their household and garden, family entertainment, General Lafayette's visit to Friendship Hill, concerns for national and international events, and probably most poignantly, the life of a New York City-bred lady isolated by the mountains from her family.

A massive task of separating fact from fiction was the first priority in all the studies done of the house by the National Park Service. The NPS has undertaken a historic resource study, general management plan, historic structure report, historic furnishings report, a study of Gallatin's influence on southwestern Pennsylvania, an industrial archaeology study of Gallatin's role in developing industry in western Pennsylvania, and a docent training manual. Similar studies available for other historic structures in the National Park Service system may help house historians understand the develpment of other houses.

The Interior of the Home

The best way to learn about a house is to spend ample time in it, preferably by living there. You can poke into closet crevices, pry above false ceilings, and investigate between floor boards to find evidence of early wallpaper, paint colors, floor coverings, and changes in room sizes. Such clues help determine how former occupants used and altered the house.

Interior Alterations

If a house has had several owners, it probably has had numerous alterations. If it was built before the twentieth century, noticeable changes will have occurred in the kitchen, bathroom, and basement areas. Other alterations may be more subtle. Look beyond new paint, soil, and scars for clues. Scraps of pink or blue wallpaper, for instance, found in the warmest room in the house may pinpoint the location of a former nursery. A strip of molding in a closet may provide the only evidence of a room's original trim. Single clues are not necessarily conclusive, but even the smallest bit of information may be significant.

Note the interior's decorative, structural, and design characteristics. Throughout the ages, styles have changed by emphasizing some details and de-emphasizing others. An awareness of design elements will help in understanding the space inside any home.

The house historian may want to become familiar with other houses built about the same time as the house under study. It is better to rely on period publications on house interiors rather than on modern decorating magazines featuring re-created period rooms. Old mail-order and trade catalogues, women's magazines, and newspapers included classified advertisements for house auctions and sales, photographs, paintings, and other contemporaneous illustrations. These publications are packed with information about actual room use, decorative items, appliances, heating and cooling systems, floor plans, and prices.

Now look at the rooms themselves. What shapes and sizes are they? Some styles stressed rectangularity with low ceilings, exposed beams, and few curves or other softening effects. Are the rooms small because they were designed for the basic needs of the family, or are they large and more spacious to accommodate leisure activities?

What are the dominant line characteristics of the room? Horizontal? Vertical? Curving? Some rooms have broad horizontal openings, such as the picture windows in twentieth-century ranch-style houses, whereas Mediterranean-inspired dwellings emphasize rounded arches, windows, and tiles. Many eighteenth- and nineteenth-century rooms accentuate verticality with high ceilings, tall windows, doors, and paneling designs. Is the room long, tall, narrow, and dark, with arched windows, a style popular during the Gothic Revival of the mid-nineteenth century, or is the room open to other spaces in the home, as well as to the outside, through large expanses of twentieth-century glass walls?

Wood, brick, stone, stucco, adobe, and plaster display various visual and tactile textures. If a rough texture is prominent in a room, does it promote a sense of earthiness? Do smooth plaster and delicate details suggest planned quiet and restraint?

Now it is time to measure, probe, prod, and analyze each room. It is useful to have on hand a flashlight, mirror, tape measure, paper and pencil,

"Aunt Floy's" parlor and bedroom suite in California in 1898 expressed her enthusiasm for decorating with great numbers of commercial and handcrafted items. Note, however, that wall-to-wall carpeting, wallpaper and paint, the same style gas fixtures, and continuous picture moldings visually unified the rooms. Where today houses might have doors or room dividers, ornamental architectural spindles and hanging beads were used. Photographs such as this are excellent documents for studying the use of interior space. Courtesy of The Bancroft Library.

dental pick, and a small, sharp knife. Occasionally more sophisticated equipment may be necessary, especially if a wall is to be taken out or samples
of wallpaper or paint colors are to be removed for professional investigation. A camera is vital for recording steps in the research and any discoveries.

The walls are a good place to start. Look closely at the architectural woodwork. Perhaps one room has more decorative trim than others in the house,
suggesting that either the room or the trim dates from the nineteenth century. At Albert Gallatin's Friendship Hill, for instance, one room has what
may be the original eighteenth-century moldings on the back windows, but
front window moldings match others in the late-nineteenth-century additions to the house.

Holes in walls may be evidence of the former locations of decorative
brackets, including those for lighting fixtures, pictures and picture moldings, curtain fixtures, cupboards, hall pieces, latches, hinges, and even wall
coverings. Old photographs of the room or illustrations of other rooms of
the period may help the researcher determine that a Victorian magazine
rack had hung at waist height or that four holes in the ceiling were for bed
curtains.

A knowledge of house styles can help the house historian identify original and replacement window openings. A room's proportions may seem wrong
because windows are too small or too large (many pre-1940 rooms were modernized with large picture windows during remodelings) for the size of the
room or wall, or do not relate to one another in size, scale, style, or molding
details. Are there similar inconsistencies on the exterior of the house? If
one or more windows are newer than others, were the older windows moved
elsewhere?

Note any unusual window shapes or any locations from which decorative
windows might have been removed. Sometimes residents concealed stained
glass windows or replaced them with clear glass when they grew tired of
the original colors. As with other decorative items, ornamental glass windows can be tied to specific time periods. Researchers should note the shape,
textures, colors, design, and location of these windows. Become familiar with
the types that were placed on stairways, in entrances, and in other areas,
and be aware that now many families collect old windows and place them
in new and old openings.

Cracks in plaster can be evidence of alterations. At Friendship Hill, a
doorway that had been closed off from a parlor was discovered from plaster
cracks that outlined an area the same size as a door opening. Tapping the

wall around and inside the cracks produced different sounds, and when a small hole was made in the plaster, framing for the doorway was found underneath. When the doorway was changed may never be known, but researchers did determine that the newer entry was less drafty than the early one near the north entrance to the home.

Sometimes the removal of a wall provides material clues to the past uses of a room. Owners of Century Inn in Scenery Hill, Pennsylvania, uncovered an original cooking fireplace that had been hidden for years behind a wall. The owners knew from the size of the chimney outside the house that a large fireplace must have been there; however, they were not prepared to find the marvelous array of early cooking utensils that had been sealed in when a modern iron stove was substituted for the earlier open hearth. Not everyone will experience such dramatic discoveries, but most houses have secrets, some, as William Seale reminds his readers in *Recreating the Historic House Interior,* located in rats' nests where "shreds of fabric, straw matting, buttons and the like" have been found.

Paints and Wall Coverings

Determining original paint colors and wallpaper is another rewarding aspect of house research. Because repainting is a relatively inexpensive way to change one's surroundings, a room may have had many colors. Each era had favorite colors, hues, degrees of brilliance (like olive green as opposed to emerald green), and tonal values (tints and shades). Many houses built in the 1950s had bathrooms with turquoise, pink, peach, black, or gray tiles and chrome accessories. Warm colors, particularly reds and oranges, were popular in the 1960s. In the mid-1980s, nineteenth-century mauves, greys, greens, and blues were revived. In many eras residents used wallpaper to enhance a room's color, design, and texture. Unfortunately, in most cases, early colors and paper can be identified only by removing the outer fabrics of the walls or part of the structural system itself, but sometimes, if walls are viewed under different lighting conditions at different times of the day, seams, edges, and even wallpaper patterns are visible.

Most early wall coverings are hidden under their modern counterparts, so more extensive investigation is needed. A flashlight and mirror are invaluable for inspecting cracks, dents, corners, areas around and under radiators, cornices, moldings, fireplaces, stairs, and large pieces of furniture such as cabinets, bathtubs, and refrigerators. Because closets are often additions to rooms and because home owners did not usually remodel closets, they sometimes contain bits of old paint colors, wallpaper, and even moldings and floorboards. Left-over paper was used to line dolls' houses, trunks, and picture frames. Some investigators have found in their attics fireboards (pieces of wood cut to fit in fireplace openings) that had been papered or painted to match the rooms where the fireboards were used.

Inspect ceiling ornaments for paint colors. Some decorative ceiling medallions were gilded, so take care while examining them. Is there any indication that the room had a decorative ceiling and that some of the pattern is still under a medallion? Could bits of wallpaper or paint colors lie hidden behind ceilings that have been lowered?

Recent sophisticated chemical and microscopic methods for determining early colors have opened our eyes to our ancestors' use of color. Rooms in George Washington's Mount Vernon now display bright Prussian blue and verdigris green, the latter color discovered under twenty layers of paint. Since builders' price lists in London indicate that verdigris green was an expensive pigment in the late eighteenth century, its use probably provides evidence of the high status of any family using it. Historians of more humble houses can learn at least which colors were available when their houses were built through old newspapers that published advertisements for pigments and paints.

If the house being researched was built before the early 1900s, or if it is a rural house, many parts of the house, both interior and exterior, may have been whitewashed. Whitewash, like light-colored paints, made rooms look brighter by reflecting candle or oil lamp light. Some families whitewashed the inside of their fireplaces after cleaning them in the spring and then stored winter bedding and clothing behind the fireboards to serve as an alternative to airing cupboards.

Removing and identifying wallpaper and paint chips are risky. The colors probably have changed because of natural aging, dirt, light, pollution, oil glazes, and linseed oil. Linseed oil, used as a binder, darkened and yellowed, changing the paint pigment with it. For some very early houses, colors have been reproduced after analyzing the clay located under or near the house. Often conservators are needed to analyze paint colors and wallpaper.

Floors and Floor Coverings

Because of continual use, floors and floor coverings contain more evidence than other areas. The house historian may be able to determine the former location of pieces of furniture or carpets by carefully examining marks, scars, or indentations in the floor. For example, a burn mark in a floor led a New Hampshire investigator to conclude that a bed had been next to the burn, which was probably created by a bed warmer. The same researcher was able to map traffic patterns in the house by analyzing how layers of floor paint had been worn away.

In order to detect subtle changes and small nail and tack holes in floors, some house historians powder their hands lightly and run them over the boards. Larger marks may lead the historian to conclusions about furniture placement. One home owner found distinctive depressions in the floor near a window. Later she learned that, years earlier, a dentist had positioned his heavy dental chair in front of the window. Another investigator learned that the wear marks on her floor were produced by the crutches of a former owner. Other marks on floors, walls, and ceilings might indicate that a wall had been removed to join two rooms. Adjacent but different board widths and placement patterns may indicate that the rooms were built at different times.

In one house, examination of the floorboards in what was believed to have been a dining room or parlor showed that several boards had been replaced. In "Historic Furnishings Report, The Cook House," published by the Junior League of Parkersburg, West Virginia, in 1984, Dolores A. Fleming wrote that the shape of the replacement area suggested that a hearth or platform for an iron cooking stove was once located there. Because the fireplace opening had been closed years before, a carpet put down, and other changes made, the present owners did not suspect that the room had been used as a kitchen until Fleming discovered the evidence in the floor and interviewed a previous owner.

Discovering a slave hole under a porch floor of a Maryland house added a poignant note to its history. The hole, less than eight-by-ten feet, and six feet deep, according to Sandra W. Justiss, a former owner of the house, had a dirt floor and walls of stone imbedded in dirt with a cage-like wooden frame to keep them from collapsing. A trap door closed the chamber. In the base of the hole, partly sunk in mud, was an early-nineteenth-century bedstead, almost completely rotted. Tax records indicated that the family owned one slave.

Floor coverings over the years include various sizes and types of floorcloths, oilcloths, straw mats, linoleum, and even sand. By the Civil War, strip carpeting was available to those who could afford it, enabling residents to cover the total floor area of a room. Holes left by tacks and nails that held down floor coverings, and a build-up of paint, shellac, or wax around the edges of earlier floor coverings are clues to their shapes and sizes. Look for bits and pieces of materials between floorboards to identify what was on the floors. While floors and floor coverings can be rich sources of information, owners of private homes and historic house museums have often obliterated evidence by sanding, waxing, and polishing wooden floors and replacing worn carpet with new.

Other Clues

House historians can date bathrooms, kitchens, and utility areas by the styles of sinks, toilets, bathtubs, cabinets, kitchen appliances, and furnaces. New technology was almost always seen first in these rooms and in the base-

In a 1942 *American Home* photograph, Armstrong Floor Covering advertised its "canteen" kitchen to appeal to war-time patriotism. The photograph illustrates a wide range of household appliances and the then-popular use of metal appliances and furnishings. Gas rationing kept people at home during the war, so Armstrong included built-in record shelves, a record player, and radio in the kitchen. Unfortunately, this black-and-white print does not catch the exuberance of the bright blues, oranges, greens, and yellows used on the towels, stools, cabinet knobs, window pulls, and floor. Photograph by the makers of Armstrong flooring.

ment. Researchers may find capped gas lines and other signs of gas lighting as well as early electrical outlets, switches, junction boxes, and lighting fix-tures. Trade catalogues, journals, mail-order catalogues, newspapers, and women's magazines can help identify changes in appliance and cabinet styles. Seemingly unimportant items provide clues to dating. For instance, house historians sometimes date bathrooms by the placement of the faucets on the wall of the sink, rather than on the shelf—a placement that was the prevailing custom before World War II and after 1960. Furthermore, researchers frequently find a date inscribed or printed under a tub or sink or on the inside of a toilet tank or lid.

Finally, consider that the house, or parts of it, may have been shipped by rail or truck to the building site. There might be manufacturers' stock numbers, letters, or names on structural elements of the house, particularly in the attic or on doorknobs, the back of woodwork, mantels, or cabinets. Often workmen signed their names on structural members or areas later covered by paint or paper. A search through local archival material may reveal the dates during which the workmen practiced their craft in the area, thus linking the construction of the house to a particular time period.

The so-called restorations of hundreds of colonial, early American, Vic-torian, and country houses that popular decorating, antique, and house maga-zines have featured for the last several decades contain many historical flaws. Our ancestors would not recognize the bright lights, exposed brick walls, highly polished floors, hanging pots, baskets, quilts, Oriental carpets, and tightly pleated "French drapes." These rooms are statements of late-twentieth-century decorating, not restorations. Recent progress in research methods, however, makes possible more honest interpretations, re-creations for house museums, and publications.

Suggested Readings

Works on the interiors of houses mentioned or quoted in this chapter are: Claudia Cook, "All the Information Is Inside: A Restored Home in Portsmouth, [New Hampshire]," in *Early American Life* 16 (February 1985): 24-29; and William Seale, *Recreating the Historic House Interior* (Nashville: American Association for State and Local History, 1979), pp. 8-9. Seale's book is a classic source for studying interiors. Sources for studying the exteriors of homes are listed at the end of chapter 2.

Architect and cultural historian Witold Rybczynski in *Home: A Short History of an Idea* (New York: Viking, 1986) traces the development over the past five hundred years of west-ern European and North American housing as it relates to notions of privacy, decoration, and function. He sees home interiors, particularly in recent centuries, becoming places where comfort was the goal and where technology—heating, plumbing, furnishings, and devices to entertain or save labor—evolved to support that goal. He is critical of modern interior design, which, he says, forgets to provide comfort.

Other relevant and useful information on ways to examine the home's interior, as well as excellent bibliographies, are found in Orin M. Bullock, Jr., *The Restoration Manual: An Illustrated Guide to the Preservation and Restoration of Old Buildings* (Norwalk, Conn.: Silvermine, 1966); Lawrence Grow and Dina Van Zweek, *A Style and Source Book: American Victorian* (New York: Harper & Row, 1984); Nigel Hutchins, *Restoring Old Houses* (New York: Gramercy, 1985); Catherine Lynn, *Wallpaper in America: The Seventeenth Century to World War I* (New York: W. W. Norton and Company, 1980); Edgar deN. Mayhew and Minor Myers, Jr., *A Documentary History of American Interiors from the Colonial Era to 1915* (New York: Scribner's, 1980); Colleen McDannell, *The Christian Home in Victorian America, 1840-1900* (Bloomington, Ind.: Indiana University Press, 1986); Richard C. Nylander, *Wallpapers for Historic Buildings* (Washington, D.C.: Preservation Press, 1983); Harold L. Peterson, *American Interiors From Colonial Times to the Late Victorians: A Pictorial Source Book* (New York: Scribner's, 1974; originally published as *Americans at Home*); Katherine Knight Rusk, *Renovating the Victorian House* (San Francisco: 101 Productions, 1982); William Seale, *The Tasteful Interlude: American Interiors Through the Camera's Eye, 1860-1917*, 2nd ed., rev. (Nashville: American Association for State and Local History, 1981); Peter Thornton, *The Domestic Interior, 1620-1920* (New York: Viking, 1984); Frank S. Welsh, *Paintpamphlet* (privately printed 1981; 859 Lancaster Avenue, Bryn Mawr, Pennsylvania); and Gail Caskey Winkler and Roger W. Moss, *Victorian Interior Decoration: American Interiors, 1830-1900* (New York: Henry Holt and Co., 1986).

Americana; American Heritage; Architecture; Bulletin of the Association for Preservation Technology; Early American Life; Journal of the Society of Architectural Historians; House Beautiful; Material Culture; The Magazine Antiques; The Old-House Journal; Victorian Homes; Winterthur Portfolio; and publications of the Pioneer America Society and Victorian Society in America often include articles about research techniques for dwellings of various eras. Technical publications are available from the American Association for State and Local History, *The Old-House Journal,* the National Park Service, and the National Trust for Historic Preservation.

Several original trade and architectural catalogues have been reprinted. Write to American Life Foundation, Box 349, Watkins Glen, New York 14891; Antiquity Reprints, P.O. Box 370-B, Rockville Center, New York 11571; Dover Books, 31 East Second Street, Mineola, New York 11501; and De Capo Press, 233 Spring Street, New York, New York 10013, for their lists. Researchers in major cities may want to contact the American Society of Interior Designers (1430 Broadway, New York, New York 10018) to see if the society has conducted Significant Interiors Surveys of houses in the area.

Newspapers, periodicals, mail-order catalogues, and builders' manuals for the era in which the house was built are particularly helpful. Long-time area residents, including those in the building and utility trades (gas service personnel know the interiors of most houses serviced by gas); local historians; architects; realtors; insurance brokers; appraisers; auctioneers; interior decorators and designers; furniture, wallpaper, paint, and carpet salespeople; and ministers are familiar with local interiors and often have information about a particular house. Also, do not forget former residents and their relatives!

·4·

Written Records

AFTER EXAMINING THE BUILDING AND ITS ENVIRONMENT, the next step for house historians is a search through written records. Most public libraries contain at least a small local history collection, and public librarians are likely to know about useful materials at nearby colleges or universities, historical societies, museums, archives, or preservation organizations.

Libraries and Archives

Among the many types of materials the house historian will want to seek out at libraries and archives are city directories, published histories, newspapers, and records of community organizations and businesses. Each type of record reveals information about local housing—information that yields valuable clues to the houses under study.

City directories are valuable to researchers because the publications include names, addresses, and occupations for most adult residents of the city. These volumes, now usually published annually, provide information on household structure by identifying spouses and adult children. Early directories often indicated race; for example, the early-twentieth-century directories of Atlanta, Georgia, printed a *(c)* next to names to indicate "colored." The same was true in northern cities at least until the Civil War and, sometimes, later. Directory listings are not uniformly complete. In some nineteenth-century directories, people had to pay to be listed, and single adult women living at home were often omitted.

In addition to alphabetical listings, most directories published after about 1915 include street indexes, listing house numbers consecutively with names of occupants and often with a symbol to indicate if the individual owned the property. A separate section categorized the business establishments in town. Finally, there may be a rural directory with individuals listed by rural route number. Scattered through the directories are ads for businesses in the community.

To trace the occupancy of a particular home, start with the current city directory and work backwards, year by year, checking the street index for the address and the name of the occupant of the property in question, then checking the name index to determine the resident's occupation. When street indexes are not included, take the last known name and check it in the previous directory, working backwards until the name no longer appears in the listings. If the building was occupied by renters, boarders, or roomers, the house historian may never be able to find the names of all the people who lived there. Such residents did not show up in ownership records and may be missed in directories published intermittently. If the address is not listed in the directory, one of two things may be true: the house may not have been built by the time the information for the directory was collected or the street name or numbering system may have been different when the information was collected.

If street indexes exist, check the addresses of other houses on the block to get a sense of the neighborhood. For example, a house may have been converted to apartments about the same time that every other house on the block was converted, it may have led the move to convert, or it may have been the last hold-out. Even if there are no street indexes, the house historian may wish to compile information for the years before house numbers were used—when residences were listed simply as "ws Jackson, 2 s Perry," which translates as a location on the "west side of Jackson, two buildings south of Perry." The next directory may show the building as the fourth house south of Perry, indicating that two new buildings were constructed in the intervening years. Paging through small-town directories for references to a particular street may be the only way to find information if names of owners or tenants are unknown.

City directories have some gaps. In small towns, editions were sporadic and sometimes editions included entries for several small towns. Very large cities may have directories back to the late eighteenth century, but not for more recent years because the cities grew too large or their residents were too transient. The last directory for Philadelphia, for example, was published for 1935-1936. Telephone directories, available for more recent years, do not include as much information as city directories.

There are limits to the usefulness of city directories. They are not error-free. Residents may say they own a house when, legally, they have only a long-term lease. Also, street names and numbering systems change, and early rural directories that listed people by postal rural route and box number may be difficult to use today.

Published histories. Researchers may find help by reading city and county histories. Almost every library will have these basic sources, which vary tremendously in quality. These works provide a context for house research but not the detail needed on a particular residence. By outlining the settlement of the state, the impact of industry, the role of war in the state's history, and the creation of transportation systems, published histories help explain the importance of specific events to the community's or city's development.

The first large-scale publication of local histories took place in the 1880s. The volumes tended to follow, especially for rural areas, a set format that concentrated first on the local topography, climate, flora, and fauna. Then, the authors discussed the Native Americans who lived in the area. Heroic stories of the early settlers were also common. Sections on local industries, schools and churches, politicians, histories of particular communities or townships, and, finally, biographical information on the important white business or civic leaders of the community, almost all of whom were male, completed the works. In a second wave of local histories between 1900 and 1920, people often paid to have their biographies included. During the 1930s, the Works Progress Administration created the Federal Writers' Project, which led to a remarkable series of local histories done by historians more interested in writing about everyday life than in providing sketches of business leaders. While some of these were published in short editions, much richer manuscript versions may be found in state or university archives by checking the American Historical Association's *Survey of Federal Writers' Project Manuscript Holdings in State Depositories.*

With the United States' bicentennial celebration in 1976, a new wave of local history publishing swept the country, to be sustained by continuing popular interest in history and the centennial, bicentennial, or even tricentennial celebrations in hundreds of towns across the nation. Local groups sometimes worked with specialized publishing companies to compile community histories, which often emphasized city or county development by focusing on specific incidents. Some families contributed their own histories. These books may be particularly useful to the house historian because they include photographs from personal collections that normally are not available in public libraries or archives.

Since the mid-twentieth century, urban historians have produced studies of particular cities. Aimed at an academic audience, these studies will help house historians understand the development of their communities. The books rarely contain references to specific homes but may provide information on city planning, development of zoning laws, growth of industry, and changing characteristics of neighborhoods.

If there is a nearby college or university with a graduate program in history, political science, urban affairs, urban planning, architectural history, or sociology, there may be a number of master's theses or doctoral dissertations available on the community or region. More than likely works will be footnoted heavily and have extensive bibliographies. The researcher may also find dissertations through *Dissertation Abstracts* at major libraries, may purchase copies of dissertations on microfilm from University Microfilms in Ann Arbor, Michigan, or may order copies through interlibrary loan from the school where the work was originally done.

Newspapers for local areas are usually found in libraries and archives, often on microfilm. For a national perspective on issues affecting housing, the historian may want to refer to the *New York Times*, established in 1851 and indexed back to its inception; the *Washington Post*, established in 1877 and indexed since 1979; the *Christian Science Monitor*, established in 1908 and indexed since 1945; and *USA Today*, established in 1982 and indexed since its first issue. The vast majority of newspapers are unindexed, making them difficult and time-consuming to use unless one knows the date of the event to be researched. However, some newspaper publishing companies have indexes, or morgues, that are open for public use.

Newspapers can help explain the context in which a house evolved by reporting the major events of the day. From their inception, American newspapers have carried real estate ads and ads for home furnishings and estate sales. The papers then broadened their coverage to include articles about neighborhoods. House historians will be interested in the real estate sections, ads for household furnishings, home improvement supplies, and notices of auctions. What prices were houses selling for at a particular time?

LAND FOR SALE.—The PLANTATION on which I lately reside, lying in Franklin County 5 miles south of Tuscumbia, containing 1,680 acres, of which 1,175 are cleared; about 70 acres in clover and grass; 26 acres are planted in the choicest fruits of every kind from Prince's Nursery on Long Island—the balance in corn and cotton. On the premises is a Brick Dwelling House 76 feet front, with two wings 42 feet, and all necessary out houses. In point of fertility of soil, health, and local advantages, it is not surpassed by any tract of land in North Alabama. For terms apply to W. A. Moseley on the premises, who is fully authorized to sell.—November 1, 1832, A. W. Mitchell. (Advertisement for Belle Mont from the Huntsville *Southern Advocate,* December 1, 1832.)

Records have shown several variations, but this is the spelling for "Belle Mont" that has been used since 1833. Comparing dimensions of the house shown in the ad with the Historic American Buildings Survey drawings of the house proved Belle Mont was the house advertised; also these dimensions are unusual in the area.

Which developers were advertising their urban rowhouses or suburban subdivisions? What did the "home" sections say about furnishings? One researcher found, for example, that a developer urged people to buy homes in his working-class subdivision in the late 1940s by linking home ownership to vigilance against communism. The researcher could contrast the promises in the ads to what she remembered from buying one of these homes after World War II. Just as some newspapers now publish annual "Progress and Industry" editions, late-nineteenth- and early-twentieth-century papers sometimes had special editions, including pictures of city scenes and articles on the city, prominent leaders, and homes.

Records of community organizations and businesses. Researchers also should look for specialized publications. Lists of middle-class and upper-class residents of the community can often be found in women's biographical books; club membership lists; records of social organizations such as country clubs; and local Social Registers, Blue Books, or elite lists. Social Registers or Blue Books include names of family members and their club affiliations. These publications may also be street indexed, thus giving the researcher a sense of the community. One can tell if club members lived in the same neighborhood, socialized at the same clubs, and worked in similar occupations. For urban areas, records of the Chamber of Commerce or manufacturers' clubs should be available from the late nineteenth century onward.

Booklets that report the festivities of a centennial celebration or histories of a church, school, club, or business can be valuable. Such booklets vary widely in size and quality, but they may provide clues to the history of a building and its occupants or to the history of the community. Histories of factories, for instance, may include information on housing built for the workers when the plant opened.

House historians may also find pamphlets that are valuable resources. Real estate promotion pieces, park publicity brochures, Chamber of Commerce or board of realtors reports, historic sites advertisements, and tour brochures can provide information on prices of homes, photographs of neighborhood recreational facilities, information on community industries and workers' homes, and photographs and information on historic houses in the area.

Diaries, journals, company records, and other manuscript sources may be useful. Owners or residents may have kept household account books, letters, or diaries that mention the building. If the home owner being researched was prominent, check the National Union Catalogue of Manuscript Collections to see if other repositories in the country have relevant material. If the individual worked for a university or corporation that has its own archives open for research, the researcher may be able to locate archival material documenting the person's worklife, particularly if the person lived in a community that was dominated by one major employer. Mortgage companies sometimes deposit in archives old records that may include information on buildings for which they held mortgages. Utility companies may have deposited records and maps indicating when gas pipe lines were laid or electric lines strung. Cemetery records may provide information on individuals. Historic property inventory forms may also have been deposited in the local library or archives.

Public Records

Public records are made or gathered by various levels and branches of government during the course of their daily business. Public records basic to house history research include plat maps, land surveyor's field notes, deeds, mortgages, liens, tax records, building permits, and public utility files. Wills and probate records pertain to both property and individuals. Among the more person-oriented public records are censuses and compilations of vital statistics. Public records often contain the sole surviving documentary evidence for a property, its owners, or residents.

The format, terminology, and complexity of public records change from jurisdiction to jurisdiction as well as over time, and their scope, number, and availability vary as well. Public records may amplify or contradict data found elsewhere. Thus, the house historian should never use public records alone, but rather with other sources.

Most indexes to public records are based on two pieces of information: a property's current legal description and a person's legal name (by law, each corporation, whether for-profit or not-for-profit, is considered to be a real person). For access to real estate records, both the property's legal description and the current owner's legal name are necessary. Although rural route and street addresses serve postal purposes, they seldom constitute the legal description used to trace a property's history. House historians can find legal names and descriptions in several places, most commonly on tax notices and deeds of transfer for the property itself. Legal names of current owners and current legal property descriptions can be obtained at the tax assessor's office, public records office, or recorder of deeds.

Usually public records list a person's name exactly as he or she normally uses it. A seldom used name or initial, however, can affect the document's placement in the alphabetical sequence of files or indexes. Names changed by marriage, divorce, partnership, or corporate reorganization may not appear in the document or its index. Indexes commonly shorten multiple owners to one name plus "et al." (and others), "et ux." (and wife), or "et vir" (and husband). Some files and indexes separate owners by categories, for example, absentee, corporate, or nonprofit.

Legal descriptions of property precisely identify real estate parcels. Traditionally, a parcel meant a single, unsubdivided tract of land. The emergence of condominium units as individually owned real estate parcels has changed this concept to include defined portions of buildings. Wording of legal descriptions varies regionally; the descriptions' importance does not.

In much of the eastern United States, early designators will be "metes and bounds" descriptions based on compass readings and natural landmarks such as streams and trees, used in conjunction with measurements of distance. For large parts of the United States, the Public Land Act of 1785 established official terminology, still in use, for a grid-like system of "sections" (one square mile), "ranges," and "townships" (thirty-six square miles). When faced with unfamilar designations, seek assistance at the office of the recorder of deeds.

Plat maps and deeds document the shape, size, legal descriptions, and ownership of land. The maps depict property boundaries and usually are filed in the office of the county surveyor, engineer, or tax assessor. Armed with a current legal description, researchers should be able to gain access to one or more plat maps, perhaps even the original land grant, for any property in the United States or Canada. The historian can use a sequentially arranged set of plat maps to identify such historical questions as when population density and land use changed faster than new boundary lines could be filed. If gaps occur in the sequence of maps, or if updates have been pasted on them, the historian may want to do sketches based on deed descriptions to fill in the missing years.

Surveyors' field notes are the basis for the legal descriptions of property. Because of different levels of competence among early surveyors and subsequent alterations to the topography, pre-twentieth-century field notes tend not to be totally reliable for modern use. Field notes provided descriptions of flora and terrain, which were used as reference points to determine boundary lines. Surveyors occasionally estimated the amount of arable and pasture lands. Although the physical features referred to may have vanished long ago, the horticultural and topographical notations help the historian get a sense of the historical landscape. Again, if adequate plat maps are not available, sketching a map from field notes provides a base to record data found later.

Measuring systems used by surveyors in their field notes have varied between regions and over time. "Chains" (66 feet), "links of chains" (100 per chain), and "perches" (units of 16 1/2 feet, also known as "poles" or "rods") were units used in early English settlements. These units were also the basis of the Public Land Survey. Spanish colonial and Mexican national governments used "varas" (33 inches), "leagues" (4,428 acres each), and "labors"

(177 acres each). This system persisted through Texas's decade as a republic and into its statehood period. Other areas under Spanish rule converted to feet and inches when they became U.S. territories. Well into the 1900s, however, New Mexicans used the word "vara" interchangeably with the 36 inch-long "yard." During the twentieth century, almost all U.S. property has been described in feet and decimals of a foot. The government offices in charge of land records, a professional surveyor, or an abstract or title insurance company can help the house historian interpret obsolete measuring systems.

A property's legal dimensions remain constant on the ground and in the public records until a need arises to change them. When a parcel is resurveyed—for subdivision, for example—its plat map is redrawn and filed with the government office responsible for local land records. Most property in contemporary subdivisions has a "description by plat." Such descriptions depend on a copy of the subdivision plat being available. Subdivision plats prepared after the mid-1940s generally contain sufficient information to re-establish the original boundary lines. Older plats, or ones in areas without strong plat laws, may lead the house historian to a dead end.

Deeds prove ownership to property. They usually are filed at a county courthouse or public records office. When arranged sequentially, deeds identify a chain of property owners. Most deed indexes are based on a "grantee-grantor" system that uses the property owners' names or on the property's legal description. Because property transfers are not necessarily between "sellers" and "purchasers," those terms can be misleading. Grantors (disposers of property) can donate property to a charitable organization, give it to a spouse or heir, or sell it. Conversely, grantees (recipients of property) can be heirs, donees, or purchasers. Both grantors and grantees can be corporations, charitable institutions, government entities, guardians or trustees, individuals, or groups.

Some historical societies have published guides to research in local deeds. Time spent learning "short cuts" that help house historians use deeds or their indexes is never wasted. Although most indexes employ an alphabetical sequence of surnames, there are countless variations. Washington, D.C., deed indexes use five systems—three based on legal names and two on legal descriptions. Each covers a different time span. In contrast, Mariposa County, Arizona, has a single grantee-grantor index that is referred to locally as "teetor" and covers all its land transactions.

Deeds include property owners' names, their places of residence, dates of property transfers, the legal description current at the time a deed was written, possible restrictions on use of the property, and the type of deed that was recorded. Deeds may detail dates of birth, marriage, divorce, or death of property owners and associated individuals. Deeds for property held in trust by a guardian may state the terms of the guardianship. Deeds of foreclosure signal financial hardship or mismanagement. Inventories of tangible assets sometimes are appended to property transfer records. Infrequently, deeds record house construction data, such as a party wall, where the property line runs through the middle of a wall.

Each deed has at least two dates: when the transaction occurred and when it was filed, or became "of record," in the recorder's office. Dates of court cases, will and probate settlements, or insanity hearings also may be included.

Deeds can help identify relationships and confusing names. Pronouns define genderless names such as Shirley and Lynn. "Jr." and "Sr." indicate kinship. While only one owner's name may appear in other public documents, the deed lists co-owners. Spellings may change dramatically over time. For example, Noah Byars, a free black property owner before the Civil War, could not read or write. His property's documents spelled his surname five ways, clues useful when researching other sources.

Deeds are key sources of women's names. If the property's grantor was a man and the body of the deed does not mention a wife, a separate dower or end statement placed near the bottom of the document may contain her name. The statements seem archaic and discriminatory, but they began as a device to protect a woman's financial interest in her husband's estate.

Deeds of trust or mortgages reveal success, bankruptcy, and sometimes an inventory of assets. These documents contain terms by which real estate is used to secure loans. Although the loan's purpose seldom is stated, the property's description, the mortgage's amount and time, and conditions of repayment almost always are included.

Deeds may contain restrictions on an owner's use of the property. Depending on the purpose and legal nuances, these portions of deeds are called "restrictive covenants" or "easements." Restrictive deeds encompass both economic and social contingencies. They can cover a specific time span or be "in perpetuity." They can provide nonowners with a right of way over property (such as limited alley access by one person or community use of a road), rights to graze cattle, or rights to use natural resources such as water.

Restrictive covenants reinforce social attitudes. Denial of land ownership

WILLOW BROOK ADDITION
RESTRICTIONS

SCALE 1"=100'

A plat map of the Willow Brook Addition. Restrictive covenants defined the type of resident developers wanted to attract to this suburb of Austin, Texas.

3901 CHERRYWOOD

During the post-World War II housing boom, subdivisions sprang up near towns and cities throughout the Unites States and Canada. Austin, Texas's capital city, was no exception. In 1946 Emmet and Jeanette Schieffer filed a subdivision plan for the farm his family had acquired fifty-nine years earlier. The tract, Willow Brook Addition, lay in the gently rolling hills northeast of Austin.

Both the subdivision and residences built in it exemplify middle-class America's thoughts on housing during that era. Despite economic growth and prosperity, the social climate was conservative. Restrictive covenants shaped Willow Brook's development, defining what was acceptable to the white middle class for which the development was intended. They established rules for use of the land itself by determining where utility service lines would run and where buildings could be placed on lots. Physical characteristics of all the buildings in the subdivision had to conform to the restrictions. Design review was vested in a committee of property owners. The restrictions also spelled out the social patterns to which owners and residents had to adhere, for example, the use of the buildings and who had the "right" to use them. Willow Brook's residents were assumed to be car-oriented, willing to commute. The subdivision contained no shopping center, church, or recreational or cultural facility.

From 1948 to 1949, the Austin-based John Broad Construction Company erected a house at 3901 Cherrywood. The house embodied the physical restrictions of the deed and the aesthetic constraints of the marketplace. Austin's climate influenced the building's design and materials. Conserving heat was less important than moderating summer temperatures. The shallow pitched gable roof was coated with adhesive, then surfaced with a light grey heat-reflecting gravel. Overhanging eaves sheltered windows from the sun, and central air conditioning was installed. Natural gas fueled the floor furnace, water heater, and range. When new, the house had minimal insulation.

The one-story, ranch-style house, built for a single family, contained two bedrooms, a bath, combination living-dining room, kitchen, and a den. A mid-twentieth-century innovation, the carport, shared the house's roof and adjoined the kitchen. Enclosed but unheated sections at the back of the carport provided storage for lawn and car equipment and laundry facilities. The flagstone patio for "outdoor living" was accessible through the den and a garden gate.

The John Broad Construction Company ceased operations after its founder died, and the disposition of its records is unknown. None of the building's inhabitants before 1970 lives near Austin; thus, public records are crucial to document the building's first two decades.

In addition, relevant public records yielded the construction company's name and years that the house was tenant-occupied. They also kept track of the street name, numbering system, and lot size, all of which changed during the first several years of the house's existence.

and residency rights because of race, religion, or national origin was prevalent in the United States for more than a century, but such written restrictions were invalidated by the U.S. Supreme Court in 1948. Restrictions also provide design control; the equivalent of zoning ordinances on height and square footage of buildings, building placement, and land use; and easements for utilities. When properties in a neighborhood, especially one that began as a suburb, share numerous physical characteristics, deed restrictions may be in effect.

Mechanics liens. Since 1833 construction industry workers have used mechanics liens to guarantee they will be paid. The liens become records of the court in which they are filed after an owner has delayed or refused payment for work accomplished. A lien specifies the person filing it, the owner of the property on which it is filed, the dollar amount it covers, and in some cases, the catalogue number of the doorbell the contractor installed. A lien remains in force until it has been paid off.

An encumbrance, widely known as a "cloud," on a real estate parcel is any condition that confuses the owner's right to the property. House historians frequently find that language within the deeds spells out any conditions of the sale. When owners fail to pay property taxes, for example, the jurisdiction to which the taxes are owed has the right to take their property.

Other encumbrances include leases, quitclaim deeds, and unprobated estates. A lease for the use of a property for the specified purpose, time, and fee must be honored even if the property changes hands. A quitclaim deed indicates that owners have agreed to give up part of the property's title to settle a boundary or ownership dispute. Because they may indicate personal, social, or economic distress, such encumbrances add to a property's history and may merit further research.

Abstract and title insurance companies compile land histories to substantiate or guarantee land ownership. The primary function of these land histories is to locate encumbrances. The companies develop elaborate sets of plat maps from pertinent maps and information abstracted from deeds. These histories are arranged chronologically for each property.

Tax records. Local or state governments levy real estate taxes based on the value of land and buildings or improvements that occupy the land. Tax records are routinely open to the general public, but tax assessors' field notes, containing detailed descriptions of buildings, may or may not be open, depending on local policy. Tax notices themselves contain at least the name of the owner of record (or owner's trustee) at the time taxes were assessed, the assessment rate, and the assessed value of the property. They also may give the owner's or trustee's address when it differs from the taxed property's and even state the building's use.

By making a chronological search through tax records, the house historian uncovers approximate dates of improvements, including new construction, major remodeling, additions, or such amenities as swimming pools, and names of owners or trustees. When the valuation method or formula remained constant between assessment dates, a significant fluctuation in the property's value from one assessment to the next usually indicates that an addition or ancillary building was erected or that damage—perhaps by fire or tornado—occurred to the property. If only the land's value differs over time, a new ordinance may have reduced or enhanced the property's marketability or the owner may have transferred some right to the land's use. If inflation or deflation is the major factor, then all adjacent properties should reflect it.

In addition, many jurisdictions have personal property tax records, which cover a somewhat different population. For example, tenants with taxable nonreal estate assets will show up on personal property tax rolls but not on real estate tax lists. Stocks and bonds and the number of gold watches or farm animals owned by the taxpayer may appear in these personal property tax records. The records' usefulness will depend on what personal assets the jurisdiction taxed and on the thoroughness and honesty of the system.

Building and occupancy permits and zoning case files may contain a wealth of structural, familial, and social data. Rural areas generally will not have such files, however, and other jurisdictions regularly discard them. If the records exist, the house historian should be able to find them at the municipal or county agency responsible for their implementation: the building inspection department, the engineer's office, or the planning commission office.

A building permit contains some or all of the following: the building's dimensions; its construction materials; whether it had a basemer t; the fuel used by its heating, ventilation, and air conditioning (HVAC) system; the names and addresses of owner, architect, and builder; any outbuildings to be constructed at the same time; the nature and rationale for any exception being allowed to the city's building code; the application and projected completion dates; and, possibly, the architectural drawings or references to historic preservation considerations such as restrictions on exterior changes. Repair permits detail the alterations they cover and sometimes state why repairs were necessary.

If permits are not available, public utility connection dates can confirm dates of construction or modernization. Unless utility records distinguish between hook-ups for new construction and existing structures, the records can be misleading and should be used cautiously.

Residential occupancy permits may exist for all housing or only for rental or multiunit buildings. The local housing authority or rent control board may use permits to ensure compliance with health and safety standards. The permits may contain any or all of the following: owners' names and addresses, property's address, size of light and air apertures, previous use, number of legal units in the building, maximum number of inhabitants allowed, date occupancy can begin, and other conditions the government deems necessary.

Zoning records relate to land use, including regulation of construction materials and methods, sizes and uses of buildings, and lot sizes. Copies of zoning ordinances or planning department regulations are usually available at public libraries or local archives. Case files for zoning appeals on individual properties contain much structural, familial, and social data. If a case was controversial, it also may have been covered by the press.

Court records. Law suits, wills and probate proceedings, and divorce and insanity cases are among the court records relevant to house historians. All court records are under the jurisdiction of the court responsible for hearing the case. If a case involving property was settled against the owner, one of the property's deeds should refer to it. If the owner won or the case was dismissed or settled out of court, the historian should seek the records of the case itself or a newspaper account. Especially important cases include

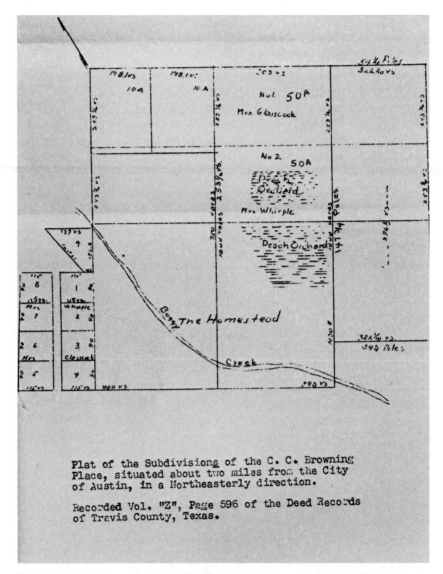

Plat of the Subdivisions of the C. C. Browning
Place, situated about two miles from the City
of Austin, in a Northeasterly direction.

Recorded Vol. "Z", Page 596 of the Deed Records
of Travis County, Texas.

This plat of the farm from which the Willow-Brook Addition was carved provides the only known documentation for the peach orchard. U.S. agricultural census records provide other details about the farm's operation.

ownership and boundary disputes, suits involving failure to fulfill construction contracts, breaking or extinguishing a restrictive deed or covenant, and
use of the property to settle a financial claim.

Wills, coupled with probate proceedings, contain the most heterogene-
ous information of all public records and are both person- and prop-
erty-oriented. House historians need to know that those who died with a
will "died testate," while those who died without a will "died intestate."
Because they describe "as is" conditions at the date of death, probate records sometimes contradict the information contained in wills. Both record
groups may provide the names and locations of heirs and partial or complete inventories of both real property and other tangibles. Probate files often
contain bills submitted to the estate's executors or administrators for expenses
incurred prior to or at death. Inventories yield both implicit and explicit
information. In one case, two of the authors researched an isolated rural
property reputed to be a local inn and stable. The inventory of the owner's
property listed only a colt, a pair of saddle bags, and three beds as relevant
items and thus cast suspicion on this story.

Divorce and insanity case files can hold information about a property.
For example, one researcher found that the records from an insanity case
that occurred during the lengthy ownership of a rural property provided the
only known description of the main house, each outbuilding's location and
use, and a list of farm animals. When court decisions in such cases have
affected the use or ownership of real estate, the property's deeds will refer
to them.

Census records are often the only means of identifying tenant populations.
The U.S. census identifies heads and sizes of households beginning in 1790
and names every occupant starting in 1850. These records are often available for at least some portion of a property's history. A few special censuses
exist such as the pre-Civil War Philadelphia Quaker documentation of free
blacks and the Oriental censuses, conducted in U.S. cities with a significant Asian population in the 1890s. Census information is not necessarily
accessible without preliminary work in other records, nor is it useful for recent
occupants. Access to manuscript returns for the federal census on individuals
is restricted for seventy-two years or, in Canada, for ninety years.

For an overview of the census and how to use it, the *Guide to Genealogical
Research in the National Archives* is a must for researchers. The guide's chap-

ter on census records describes the contents of each census and lists all states and territories covered. It also describes special agriculture and manufacturing enumerations, both of which have merit for the house historian working on a rural or mixed-use property.

In addition to specific data about a building's residents, census records provide a basis for comparison. The house historian can draw conclusions about the relative well-being of a family; the presence of boarders or lodgers; whether areas had high concentrations of ethnic or minority group members; an individual's geographic mobility; and, for women listed in the 1900 census, the mortality rate of their children. Once a property's residents have been located in the census, surrounding entries provide comparable information about neighbors. Other facts may appear as well. For example, the impact of bad weather on farm land can be seen in agricultural census reports. To gain an even more complete picture, the researcher may want to correlate data from the census with data from other sources, such as city directories.

Compilations of vital statistics—birth, marriage, divorce, and death records—are kept by state governments. They may be available at the county courthouse in an abbreviated register, but in some states their use is restricted by "right to privacy" legislation. Difficult to obtain without full names and the date of the event involved, vital statistics provide information about inhabitants, rather than the residence itself. House historians can use vital statistics to confirm dates, however. For example, if the record states that a birth or death occurred at a given address, it verifies a building's existence at that address and at that date.

Other public records may be relevant. Fire department log books outline the extent of fire damage to a building, and city inspectors' annual reports usually enumerate, by type, residences built within a given year. Post office records show the date a rural postal route began, the condition of nearby roads, and perhaps which farmhouse was used as a community post office. To locate these records, the historian's best ally may be a librarian, architect, local historian, county clerk, or the city's oldest postal employee.

With such an array of sources, the house historian will never find a home about which no information exists. More likely than not, public records will be the backbone for a full-blown "tell us everything there is to know" house history.

Suggested Readings

For guidance in locating and using published and unpublished local history sources, see the relevant chapters and bibliographies in Kyvig and Marty, *Nearby History*. Other important sources are Clifford L. Lord, ed., *Localized History Series* (New York: Bureau of Publications, Teachers College, Columbia University, 1964-1971); C. S. Peterson, *Bibliography of County Histories of the 3,111 Counties in the Forty-Eight States* (Baltimore: Clarence Peterson, 1946); and Marion J. Kaminkow, ed., *United States Local Histories in the Library of Congress*, 5 vols. (Baltimore: Magna Carta, 1975). Local libraries may have specialized bibliographies of sources for their areas. The Fall 1983 issue of *The Public Historian* provides an excellent summary of the history of writing local history that can guide researchers.

To help beginning researchers, AASLH has published a series of technical leaflets including "Early American Account Books: Interpretation, Cataloging, and Use," by Robert J. Wilson, III, AASLH Technical Leaflet 140, *History News* 36:9 (September 1981), "Local History Manuscripts: Sources, Uses and Preservation," by Nancy Sahli, AASLH Technical Leaflet 115, *History News* 34:5 (May 1979), "Methods of Research for the Amateur Historian," by Richard W. Hale, Jr., AASLH Technical Leaflet 21, *History News* 24:9 (September 1969), and "Using Memoirs to Write Local History," by Elizabeth Y. Enstam, AASLH Technical Leaflet 145, *History News* 37:11 (November 1982).

For information on newspaper sources, check the state archives or the state historical society to see if a newspaper project sponsored by the National Endowment for the Humanities is underway in the state. These projects are producing computerized bibliographies of known newspapers in several states.

Sources for newspapers include *American Newspapers, 1821-1936: A Union List of Files Available in the United States and Canada* (New York: H. W. Wilson, 1937) and *Newspapers in Microform: United States, 1948-1983* (Washington, D.C.: Library of Congress, 1984). Several major regional newspapers have been indexed for recent years. These include the Boston *Globe*, Denver *Post*, Houston *Post*, Los Angeles *Times*, New Orleans *Times-Picayune*, St. Louis *Post-Dispatch*, San Franciso *Chronicle*, and St. Paul *Dispatch and Pioneer Press*. The Canadian Newspaper Index began in 1977 and indexes seven English-language Canadian newspapers, including the Toronto *Globe* and *Mail*. The *Budget* is a weekly newspaper serving Amish and Mennonite communites across the country. Published since 1889, it includes information on agriculture, weather, barn raisings, and house raisings from correspondents in each community.

Chadwyck-Healey, Inc., has produced a "National Inventory of Documentary Sources in the United States," which consists of microfiched finding aids, registers, and collection guides in repositories throughout the United States. The four-part series includes "Federal Records: The National Archives, the Presidential Libraries, and the Smithsonian Institution Archives," "Manuscript Division, Library of Congress," "State Archives, State Libraries, and State Historical Societies," and "Academic and Research Libraries and Other Repositories." Because of cost, this series likely will be available only at major research libraries.

The Historic Records Survey conducted as part of the Works Progress Administration in the 1930s uncovered records in courthouses, city halls, and other government offices across the country. Check with a major archives in the state to see where survey records are kept. During the 1930s, the WPA conducted interviews with former slaves. These interviews provide a rich source on slavery and the lives of slaves.

A particularly useful guide is the *Survey of Federal Writers' Project Manuscript Holdings in State Depositories* by Ann Banks and Robert Carter, which provides a "comprehensive guide to all extant manuscripts, indexed by state." The guide, published in 1985, is available through the American Historical Association, 400 A Street, S.E., Washington, D.C. 20003. It gives references for every state except Alaska, Hawaii, and Michigan; records for Puerto Rico have not yet been located, and those of Maine and Rhode Island are sketchy.

Except for genealogical publications, literature about local public records has been scant and is often out of print. Even when available, the literature rarely address documentation of individual houses. One exception is Nina Fletcher Little's classic "Finding the Records of an Old House," *Old Time New England* 40 (October 1949).

State archives and historical societies have prepared guides to local records. Some focus on records pertaining to the built environment. Donald Dean Parker's *Local History: How to Gather It, Write It, and Publish It* (New York: Social Science Research Council, 1944) contains a chapter on public records. Much of the information remains valid. However, Parker does not discuss the relevance of the records to a specific building, nor does he address such sources as building permits and zoning regulations. Kyvig and Marty's *Nearby History* covers some of the same records as Parker's book.

AASLH Technical Leaflet 55, "Glossary of Legal Terminology: An Aid to Genealogists," by Shelby Myrick, Jr., in *History News* 25:7 (July 1970), is also valuable. Other useful technical leaflets are: "Black Genealogy: Basic Steps to Research," by Bill R. Linder, AASLH Technical Leaflet 135, *History News* 36:2 (February 1981), and "Jewish Genealogy: An Annotated Bibliography," by Malcolm H. Stern, AASLH Technical Leaflet 138, *History News* 36:5 (May 1981).

The most comprehensive overview of public records in the United States is the *Guide to Genealogical Research in the National Archives* (n.p.: n.p., 1983). Despite its reference to genealogists, the guide covers almost all of the National Archives's record sets useful to house historians. It is the definitive source on the contents of each federal census open for general research. *Tracing Your Ancestors in Canada*, by Patricia Kennedy and Janine Roy (Public Archives of Canada, rev. 1984), is available through the Minister of Supply and Services; it provides excellent information on land records and vital statistics.

American Jurisprudence, second edition, is the best legal encyclopedia. The house historian interested in more than dictionary definitions of legal terminology should look for *Am Jur*, as it is called informally, at the public or law library or a law firm in the area. Summaries of significant local court cases may appear in each state's multivolume edition of the *Reporter Annotated*, published variously.

Public records undergird research in urban history, housing, and family life. James Oliver Horton and Lois E. Horton relied heavily on census data for their chapter "Families and Households in Black Boston" in *Black Bostonians* (San Francisco: Holmes & Meier, 1979). Papers presented at local historical society meetings and research on local or social history draw heavily on public records. Available in some archives or libraries, these studies can be used to compare an individual house's family structure, size, and cost to others built at the same time.

"The players" and "the rules" of municipal zoning are discussed in Richard F. Babcock, *The Zoning Game* (Madison: University of Wisconsin Press, 1966).

·5·

Oral and Visual Sources

ORAL HISTORY INTERVIEWS TAP THE MEMORIES OF INDIVID-
uals acquainted with a building, thus giving the house historian access to
first-hand knowledge about it. Who can better explain why a tenant rented
a particular apartment than the tenant him- or herself?

According to Barbara Allen and Lynwood Montell in *From Memory to
History: Using Oral Sources in Local Historical Research*, information obtained
in oral history interviews supplements written records, complements formal
histories, and provides information that exists in no other form. For example, one city's published history describes civic improvements that made
indoor plumbing possible but says nothing about how quickly bathrooms
became the norm or how long and why an individual building stood without plumbing. City records provide dates of hook-ups but do not reveal the
impact of indoor plumbing on residents. During one oral history interview,
an interviewee vividly related his great-grandmother's description of the installation of her family's bathroom, the first in its neighborhood. He also remembered that the ancestor invited neighborhood girls to her "bathtub" parties
(similar to present day slumber parties), seemingly trivial information that
not only reveals social impact but also the personalities of the house's
residents.

Oral history interviewing requires preparation. A guide such as Willa K.
Baum's *Oral History for the Local Historical Society* is essential. Most important to a successful interview is the development of a framework or outline
of topics to be covered during the interview. Based on research done elsewhere, the outline includes names, dates, significant events and objects, as
well as information gaps.

Oral history provides the only nonartifactual documentation that John Rutledge "wintered over" his bees in the garage's heated loft. Note the loft's opening for the bees and the garages's board and batten siding.

Each interview has its own set of goals. For instance, historic preservationists may want to ask about structural details, facts that are often omitted from formal histories, especially as physical tests of a building are not always feasible or, indeed, possible. For example, the plaster could be too important to remove or evidence may have been lost in alterations. Oral history may be the only remaining route of historical investigation. To obtain structural information, likely interviewees include architects, builders, or craftsmen associated with the property's construction or repairs.

An ideal way to obtain information about a house is to conduct an on-site walk-around interview while carrying a portable tape recorder, the building's floor plan, and a landscape plat. As the interviewee identifies each room and outdoor physical feature, the interviewer can record that information directly on the plan, plat, and tape. Artifacts associated with the property can stimulate the memories of interviewees. Every item, be it an individual piece of furniture in a walk-up apartment or an entire country estate, is an artifact, a "thing of history," to use historian David J. Russo's term. These "things" make historical statements. A crank telephone, for instance, implies a farm owner's need or desire for rapid communication with the outside world.

Fragments of family, ethnic, or cross-cultural tradition also emerge from the oral history interview. An interviewer may learn that a family opens presents on Christmas Eve rather than Christmas Day, a custom that may be the sole remnant of a German ancestor's influence. In a contemporary apartment in the Midwest, an interviewer may find out that the Old South custom of eating black-eyed peas on New Year's Day to bring good luck occurs annually during a bowl game party.

Oral history and folklore often appear intertwined. Friendship House, the subject of the case study on pages 72-74, has a ghost tradition, for example. The unmarried sister of the first owner died about the time her brother went bankrupt. Local folklore holds that her ghost wanders through the house, wringing her hands, and looking for the lovely lost furnishings.

Folklore does not belong to any geographic area or educational or economic strata. If a fraction of the East Coast's colonial houses alleged to have been built of brick "imported from England" had been so, the Atlantic Ocean would have been crowed with ships carrying brick. Buried treasure, heroic acts, and "hanging trees" are other folklore elements. Folklore related during an interview enhances the house's history. Richard Dorson, a nationally known folklore scholar, cites such potential "enrichment of the historical narrative" as a key attraction of local history research.

Hilly Grove Farm

Hilly Grove Farm consists of 290 acres located on the shore of Lake Huron, Ontario, Canada. A part of Manitoulin Island, the farm encompasses one-half mile of bay shore frontage, timber land (or "bush" as Canadians call it), marshes, wet and dry pastures, planting fields, a gravel deposit, and sizeable limestone outcroppings.

Approximately 6,000 Ojibway and 7,000 Anglo-European descendants composed the island's 1985 population. All of the island was Indian Reserve from 1836 to 1862. When an 1862 treaty opened the island to white settlers, Native Americans retained control of the eastern end.

John Rutledge, one of the many early purchasers, migrated from southern Ontario. He bought several parcels and began the farm now known as Hilly Grove. The farm's primary structures are the original farmhouse—a one-and-a-half-story log cabin built about 1870; a newer log and frame house; a twentieth-century board and batten construction garage; and the farm's largest structure, the barn built in 1903. Corrals, stock fences, and pens are made of logs or split rails cut on site.

Members of the Rutledge family owned and occupied the farm until 1942 when it became a tenant farm for a nearby merchant. When a U.S. citizen purchased the farm in 1967, he continued to rent the land and barn and made the older log cabin a summer residence. He also installed the farm's first electricity, a pump for the old artesian well, indoor plumbing, and a septic field. The newer house is vacant, but stabilized.

A walk-around interview with Hilly Grove's owner yielded information on twenty years of previously undocumented physical change. For example, after the original log cabin was moved to allow a public road to be widened, a rear section was added to the cabin. Its exposed rafters are cedar logs cut from island trees. The owner insisted on leaving their bark intact, despite the local building contractor's disapproval. For several years, the logs were home to bugs, and little sawdust piles formed under the logs as the contractor had predicted—a small price to pay, according to the owner. This portion of the interview explained the cabin's relocation and its unusual construction technique in a community with strong local building traditions.

For years, the church abutting the farm has served only as a place to hold funerals and memorial services. A question about the church prompted another interviewee to describe two other institutions that once stood nearby and the old community they served. The interviewee explained that the farm traditionally was called "The Rutledge Farm,"

Hilly Grove's log cabin. The room to the right of the front door is the one identified in the case study as the post office.

Second and third generation owners of Hilly Grove Farm. When the little boy was an infant, his four older siblings died within an eleven-day period, an event that has become part of the local oral tradition. His mother's dark clothing probably represents the "deep mourning," which would have been appropriate for a minimum of two years after her children's deaths.

but that one room of the log cabin had served as the post office for the community of Hilly Grove. Although the interviewee assumed she was relating common knowledge, local history booklets make no reference to the community or its institutions.

Documentation for both the community and the farm is fragmented. The Assiginack Historical Museum in Manitowaning has a small collection of Rutledge family artifacts. Most of Manitoulin's local history has been carried on through oral tradition, a tradition reinforced by intermarriages between island families and by geographic separation from the mainland. In 1983 publication began of *"Through the Years, a magazine dedicated to the recording of Manitoulin District history."*

The farm's physical documentation includes its buildings, gravel pit, cattle trails, construction date chiseled on a foundation stone of the barn, and the old crank telephone in the newer house. Land records and wills provide names of owners, mineral leasing agreements, and legal information. Other data must be obtained from tombstones in the community cemetery, oral history interviews, and what few family papers survive.

The oral history interviewees for this case study included the owner, long-time island residents, and a relative (by marriage) of the Rutledges. Each contributed unique information. One "fact" led to a search in the Canadian National Archives postal records, which confirmed Hilly Grove's use as a post office and provided dates of that use and the names of Rutledge family members who had been appointed postmasters. Other "facts" sent the researcher back to previous interviewees as well as to the public records to confirm or correct information previously gathered.

Material for this case study was abstracted from an unpublished report containing data gathered with the cooperation of Austin Beall, owner of Hilly Grove Farm; Jeanne Dixon; Pearl Hall; and the Assiginack Historical Museum.

Visual Documents

Photographs, paintings, maps, architect's drawings, and other graphic materials yield details not included in other sources. The graphic artifact itself provides corroborative documentation. For example, if an 1850's daguerreotype of a building exists, the historian can assume that the structure was standing before the Civil War. Dated maps, photographs, and drawings not only confirm a structure's existence at a given time, but also frequently show dimensions, building styles, and materials.

Maps are useful forms of visual documentation. Every part of the United States has been mapped in one way or another, so every structure should have at least one map associated with it. Perhaps the most familiar types of maps are those used with legal descriptions of property, subdivision maps, individual plot maps, or plat plans. These documents establish the overall dimensions of the property and sometimes those of the house and related structures as well.

Modern mapping techniques rely heavily on aerial photography to measure the earth's surface quickly and accurately. Maps made from aerial photography are valuable to house historians because they show land use patterns, the relationship of buildings to nearby geographic features such as streams, and the arrangement of buildings on the land. Aerial photographs produced by government agencies are available at a modest cost. For further information, contact the state geological survey or soil conservation service.

By the mid-1800s, insurance companies were producing maps that contained information about the built environment. Agents consulted these maps when writing insurance policies and adjusting claims and provided copies of maps to fire companies. Insurance maps contain street names and addresses; sizes of buildings and descriptions of the buildings' placement on lots; types of construction materials and number of stories of both primary and ancillary buildings. Other notations indicate the location of fire alarm boxes and water sources and perceived fire hazards, such as heating systems that could explode and windows barred to prevent access. Local libraries, real estate offices, and title insurance firms are the best sources for Sanborn fire insurance maps, which were published periodically from 1867 to 1950.

Somewhat different in function are published plat maps and county atlases.

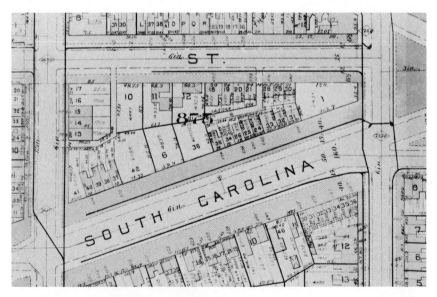

By examining a series of atlases for a particular urban area, house historians can learn the approximate dates that large tracts were subdivided, the sizes and shapes of the subdivided lots, and the approximate dates that buildings first appeared on them. After the 1880s, Friendship House's "grounds," all of block 875, were subdivided to create lots 13 through 41.

These books depict scattered buildings or less densely populated neighborhoods outside of "fire zones"—buildings that may not appear on insurance maps of densely settled areas. Plat books usually show civic improvements such as paved streets and utility lines; atlases show rural road locations—all aids to analyzing a home's relationship to its general environment.

Maps created by the U.S. Geological Survey (USGS), formerly the U.S. Coast and Geodetic Survey, cover the entire nation. The maps are extremely important to historians documenting rural property because they show individual structures. These topographic maps are updated periodically, so the changes they document can be compared over time. USGS maps also provide the necessary coordinates to "site" a building for nomination to the National Register. Researchers may purchase these maps from state geological survey offices or use them at regional repositories throughout the country. Other U.S. government maps are available, such as census enumeration district maps and postal route maps, which show delivery routes, post offices, and sometimes the names of individuals who lived along the routes.

Some maps help the historian fill in details of historical context. If a home's occupants commuted to work, for instance, look for transportation company maps showing commuter routes and major transfer points. Maps prepared for anniversary celebrations reveal how a town or neighborhood wanted to present itself and its buildings. By comparing a 1952 promotional map indicating historic houses on Capitol Hill in Washington, D.C., with the status of the neighborhood today, the historian will see that more than one-third of the residences designated on the map as historic have been demolished. Moreover, only one of the historic district's notable Victorian bay front rowhouses was even listed.

Architectural plans and drawings are, in a sense, maps of a building. They provide specific measurements and information on materials and locate structural, mechanical, and other features, some of which are hidden. Plans and drawings are more apt to exist for buildings designed by architects or major developers or if the building is a catalogue house or prefabricated house. Drawings may be found in the possession of the owner; descendants of the original owner; the family, firm, or alma mater of the building's architect or builder; or in a library or archives, or an attic.

Architectural drawings may include renderings of facades, floor plans, cross sections, electrical plans, and many other design elements. Depictions of elevations and facades illustrate the exterior of a building and often give

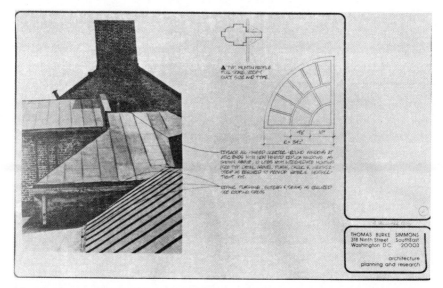

Many late-twentieth-century "blueprints" are blue in name only. They also depart from the traditional form of using line drawings exclusively by integrating photographs with drawings and text. This sheet is from the project documentation of a 1978 rehabilitation by Thomas Burke Simmon, AIA.

dimensions of windows, doors, and other features. Floor plans, which are, in essence, maps of the horizontal surface, show spatial relationships among walls, windows, doors, and stairs and frequently designate room usage. Cross sections, vertical maps of interior spaces, reveal wall and floor construction details and height. Other architectural drawings show central heat and air systems, water and plumbing systems, and electrical services. Detail sheets illustrate window frames, carved keystones, moldings, and other ornamental and functional elements. A complete set of drawings also may include landscape plans.

The importance of preserving architectural documents for historic structures was recognized in 1933 by the establishment of the Historic American Buildings Survey (HABS). This unit of the National Park Service produces archival photographs, measured drawings, and brief histories of selected buildings throughout the nation. The collection, permanently on file at the Library of Congress, provides a data base to compare the physical characteristics of buildings. Catalogues based on the collection have been published for some states and cities.

Photographs and artwork. Photographs are often the most accessible visual materials available for structures built after the 1850s. Grand or historic buildings are more likely to have been photographed before 1900, but with the advent of the Kodak box camera in the 1890s, photography became a popular hobby, and homes were a primary subject.

Photographs and architectural drawings complement each other. Comparing the two sources reveals a third set of data. For example, if design changes occurred during construction, they may not be reflected in architectural drawings but will appear in "as built" photographs. Photographs of cross sections of buildings are rare, and the camera is unable to produce floor plans. Specifications for wallpaper and other interior design elements are not always included in architectural plans, but interior photographs can provide the historian with details of these elements.

Researchers often find period photographs of homes in family albums, newspaper offices, professional photographic studios, and private or public collections. Promotional documents advertising a subdivision or town may contain clear photographs of identifiable houses. When photographs and drawings do not exist, the historian may have to rely on views of nearby buildings with the same general characteristics to get a sense of what "might have been." Many homes contain elements, such as lighting fixtures, mantels, and doors, ordered from catalogues or merchants whose stock was depicted in city directories and newspaper advertisements.

Sometimes a photograph taken to document something other than the building will reveal design details. A magnifying glass may help the historian look for details or verify an alteration.

On a more sophisticated level, photogrammetry has emerged in the last few years as an invaluable tool for preservationists and house historians. Providing detailed visual information, modern photogrammetry measures three dimensions photographically. The technique must be done by professionals with sophisticated equipment to be accurate. You can locate a professional through the State Historic Preservation Office.

As a methodology, photogrammetry closely resembles stereographs in which a pair of images produces a single, seemingly three-dimensional picture. Thus, if two photographs are taken of an object, either with two cameras or by one camera from two different positions, so that the resulting photographs overlap, the resulting "stereo pair" can be viewed in "three dimensions" with the proper device. This process also produces "as is" measured drawings for

This nineteenth-century home in central West Virginia was recorded by close-range photogrammetry, using a Wild C120 stereo metric camera. This photograph shows one-half of the Cunningham House; the "targets" on the porch pillars help the photographer establish a base for the correct scale of the photograph. The recording was done under a contract from the U.S. Army Corps of Engineers—Huntington District. The preliminary drawing of the Cunningham House (opposite page, top), plotted on a Wild A40 autograph, shows the house "as is," with the preservationist's comments on changes to be made. The final drawing of the Cunningham House (opposite page, bottom) reflects the corrections noted on the previous drawing. This sketch was then given to the architect to illustrate how the renovated building should look when completed.

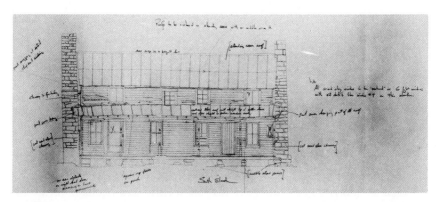

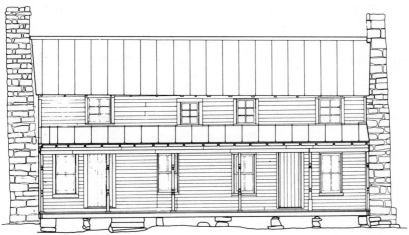

house historians. The process is rapid, versatile, and more accurate than hand measurements.

During the last quarter of the nineteenth century, itinerant artists roamed America to produce "bird's-eye views" of almost every town. Artists of varying degrees of skill occasionally portrayed homes in oils, watercolors, or etchings, although they may have exercised a certain freedom of interpretation. For example, a drawing of Friendship House shows bricks laid in running bond when, in fact, the bond is Flemish. Works of art can be found at galleries, antique shops, auctions, and in private and public archives. They may also be published as illustrations in local history books or atlases.

Visual documents are critical to understanding the history of a home. They can supplement, clarify, and correct the written record or stimulate the memories of individuals being interviewed for oral histories. Photographs, floor plans, or sketch maps prepared while researching a house history will become important artifacts in their own right—part of the house's history for future researchers.

Friendship House
The Maples

Friendship House, formerly named The Maples, is the oldest known privately owned residence extant on Capitol Hill in Washington, D.C. William Mayne Duncanson, an Englishman who had amassed a fortune in India, arrived in the new capital about 1795. He bought unimproved lots throughout the city, then selected an entire block on Capitol Hill to be his town estate. A friend of George Washington and Thomas Jefferson, Duncanson planned to entertain in a grand manner. William Lovering, Duncanson's architect, designed a substantial two-story brick Federal-style house, typifying the environment that the social and political elite of early Washington strove to create. The main building sits on a hill, back from the street. Newspapers and private documents referred to the building soon after it was completed and confirm a construction date of 1796 to 1797. Unfortunately, Duncanson was forced into bankruptcy by 1800 and lost his entire estate.

Nineteenth-century owners included U.S. Senator John Clayton and Emily Edson Briggs, a leading journalist. Each left a mark on the building. Clayton, for example, added a ballroom and installed gas heating and lighting in 1856, a fact corroborated by a dated gas line discovered during a 1978 archaeological dig.

The Maples outlived its original function. In 1937 Washington architect

Harold Mansfield, a member of the construction crew for Friendship House's 1937 adaptive use altera-tion, shot this excellent sequence. The top photograph shows the house the day before gutting began; Friendship House staff members visit the site during rehabilitation (middle); the work completed (bot-tom). The porch and shutters have never been replaced; only photographs and blueprints document their existence.

Horace Peaslee removed almost all the exterior trim and alterations and designed flanking symmetrical wings. He created a new entrance through the rear of the property and developed a playground in the original front yard.

Now known as "Friendship House," the building houses a social service organization. Begun in 1904, Friendship House was the first settlement house in Washington and has an extensive history of its own. By the 1950s, its location was at the center of Washington's "back to the city" movement.

Balancing the functions of a public service agency with the maintenance needs of a 200-year-old building listed on the National Register of Historic Places has been a delicate task for Friendship House's board of directors. Despite a slender budget, the organization strives for exterior stabilization and maintenance to be consistent with the Secretary of the Interior's *Standards for Rehabilitation and Guidelines for Rehabilitating Historic Buildings.* At the same time, the building's grounds and interior must endure the heavy traffic of its client population. Portions of the building have been made accessible to the handicapped in recent years.

Friendship House is relatively well documented. For instance, public records include a loan Duncanson obtained prior to his bankruptcy that was secured by all of his household furnishings. During the 1930s, HABS prepared measured drawings of the building and a short history was compiled from secondary sources for its National Register nomination. Additional information has been garnered from primary sources to justify historic preservation grants and from an archaeological dig supported by a U.S. Department of the Interior grant in conjunction with volunteers from a Smithsonian Associates program.

No pre-1937 written description exists for Friendship House's building. Without the available visual sources, house historians and historic preservationists would have to rely solely on the extant physical attributes. Thus, they could only guess at the size and shape of the nineteenth-century wings, which Peaslee removed, and would have little inkling of the original gradations of the surrounding yard, the location of the drive, or even the existence of servants' quarters.

Suggested Readings

A general guide to the practice of oral history is Willa K. Baum's *Oral History for the Local Historical Society*, 2nd ed., rev. (Nashville: American Association for State and Local History, 1977). Oral history sources are included in Kyvig and Marty's "Oral Documents" chapter in *Nearby History*. Barbara Allen and Lynwood Montell's *From Memory to History: Using Oral Sources in Local History Research* (Nashville: American Association for State and Local History, 1981) discusses the use of artifacts in conjunction with oral history. For an overview of how artifacts and "orally communicated history" affect historical research, see David J. Russo's article "'The Things' of History" in *Canadian Review of Studies* 15 (1984).

Richard M. Dorson's *American Folklore and the Historian* ((Chicago: University of Chicago Press, 1971) details the interdisciplinary action between folklore and history. Dorson's classic textbook is *American Folklore* (Chicago: University of Chicago Press, 1959). Folklore scholarship has produced abundant literature for most geographic areas in North America as well as most topics. Relevant periodicals include *Journal of American Folklore, Western Folklore, Southern Folklore Quarterly*, and *New York Folklore Quarterly*. To check oral tradition for specific folklore influence, refer to *Funk & Wagnall's Standard Dictionary of Folklore, Mythology, & Legend*, edited by Maria Leach and Jerome Fried (New York: Harper & Row, 1984).

For general information on the use of maps as sources, see Kyvig and Marty, *Nearby History*, pp. 73-86. USGS map information is in Robert M. Vogel's heavily illustrated "Quadrangular Treasure: The Cartographic Route to Industrial Archeology," in *IA: The Journal of the Society for Industrial Archeology* 6 (1980): 25-54.

Fire Insurance Maps in the Library of Congress: Plans of North American Cities and Towns Produced by the Sanborn Map Company (Washington, D.C.: Library of Congress, 1981) is the basic guide to these maps. Microfilm copies of Sanborn maps are available from Chadwyck-Healey, Inc.

Index maps of each state, a pamphlet describing the maps, and information on acquiring USGS may be obtained from the U.S. Geological Survey, Distribution Section (1200 South Eads Street, Arlington, Virginia 22202) for areas east of the Mississippi River, Puerto Rico, and the Virgin Islands. The Federal Center (Denver, Colorado 80225) provides information on areas west of the Mississippi River. Canadian maps can be obtained from the Canada Map Office, Department of Energy, Mines & Resources (615 Booth Street, Ottawa, Ontario K1A OE9).

Information on census enumeration districts is found in the *Guide to Genealogical Research in the National Archives* (n.p.: n.p., 1983), pp. 255-261.

A technical work on remote sensing is *Remote Sensing: A Handbook for Archeologists and Cultural Resource Managers* by Thomas R. Lyons and Thomas Eugene Avery (Washington, D.C.: National Park Service, 1977); it includes a bibliography on historical geography and archaeology and a glossary.

For further information on historical photographs and techniques for taking photographs, see Kyvig and Marty, *Nearby History*, pp. 128-148. A standard work on architectural photography is Jeff Dean, *Architectural Photography: Techniques for Architects, Preservationists, Historians, Photographers, and Urban Planners* (Nashville: American Association for State and Local History, 1981).

·PART II·
Interpreting the Clues

·6·

Achieving the American Dream in Housing

"IT MAY NOT BE PRETTY, BUT IT'S HOME" SYMBOLIZES Americans' attachment to houses. Our love affair with our homes has been more than an individual dream. Outside pressures have been strong and persuasive. A home was to provide protection, culture, and morality. Government policies, social reform movements, financial institutions, real estate speculators and developers, advertisements, popular magazines and songs, novels, movies and television programs, and builders' manuals have influenced and reflected feelings about owning a house. Even in the early decades of the seventeenth century, the single-family dwelling was the norm, despite the dangers of attacks from Native Americans and the extremes of weather, which might have made multifamily houses more practical. Except in densely settled urban areas, this pattern persists.

Acquiring the Land

Without land grants there would be no American dream. European governments started the tradition when they awarded large tracts of land to encourage settlement in the colonial period. Original grantees then subdivided their holdings, and the individual house on a plot of ground quickly became the preferred choice. Implementing its own policy of land grants, the United States government offered frontier land to its Revolutionary War veterans. Many veterans rushed west, some as far as the Mississippi River, to claim their individual parcels; still others sold their land, sight-unseen, to real estate speculators. The Republic of Texas copied federal practice by

79

awarding land to soldiers who fought in its revolution in 1836. To encourage settlement of the Great Plains, the United States government enacted the Homestead Act of 1862. Whenever the frontier moved, settlers who did not purchase their land or receive direct grants staked claims by planting crops, building houses, or marking their boundaries. In these regions, land ownership records tend to be complex.

Inheritance practices also contributed to American housing patterns. Because property usually is divided rather than going to the eldest son, family homes have not passed down through generations as they have in England. In each generation, newly fashionable dwellings have been built, leaving the parental home to others or to the wrecking ball.

The Colonial Era

Colonial North American cities clustered at water's edge. Streets were narrow and lots small, with buildings placed so close together that inhabitants could reach any portion of their compact city by walking. Most of the city's residents lived in rowhouse dwellings. In major cities such as Philadelphia and Boston, the wealthiest residents copied European ideas that fashionable, respectable urban addresses were near the center of town. The farther a resident lived from that center, the more likely the person was to be poor. Southern cities deviated from this pattern by having a broader population mix near their centers. There, slaves and free blacks lived close to their owners and employers.

Urban dwellings routinely contained small manufacturing and business enterprises; buildings whose primary function was business, such as mercantile and printing establishments, often had living spaces for apprentices. Except for government or institutional buildings, differences of style, materials, and scale were so limited that the generic word "house" almost never appeared alone. Buildings were categorized by primary function rather than by form or location; thus, the word "house" was usually preceded by "school," "meeting," or "dwelling."

Early public and private efforts to control housing began in the cities. Concerned about public safety, governments regulated building materials for houses, primarily to prevent the spread of fires. After several disastrous seventeenth-century fires, Boston banned wooden chimneys. Some early building codes prohibited reed and straw roofing, wood and plaster chimneys, and wooden buildings in urban centers. Rural and small town dwellings continued to reflect European ideas and will be dealt with in the next chapter.

The Nineteenth Century

The Industrial Revolution created new jobs in both old and new American cities. New technologies, including the construction of public utilities, mass transportation systems, and the perfection of balloon-frame housing, generated a demand for immigrant labor. Consequently, cities grew rapidly and became dirty and overcrowded.

By the early nineteenth century, most American cities had suburban slums reminiscent of those in Europe. Beyond the slums, out into rural areas, country estates of the wealthy provided a respite from urban dust and noise and established a pattern of luxury that whetted middle-class appetites for nonurban living. Early in the nineteenth century new land use patterns developed in Boston and New York, with suburbs as the home of the upper-middle class and middle-class and the inner city for the poor and the very rich. In the 1850s, Alexander Jackson Davis designed the first "picturesque" suburb, Llewellyn Park, for wealthy New York City businessmen who commuted by train from the New Jersey countryside. Other suburban developers soon created less expensive versions near expanding mass transportation systems. The deteriorating quality of city housing for the poor became a private, then a governmental concern. Beginning in 1867, New York City legislators passed laws on housing reform, a movement that was emulated across the country.

The Spread of House Designs

The American house became an important force in shaping cultural values. In seventeenth-century Puritan New England, the adornment of a house had been frowned upon; houses in other colonies were relatively modest as well. In the eighteenth century, however, refined Georgian-style houses symbolized personal success, social position, and security. By the nineteenth century, many believed that the industrious man could acquire a proper home and by doing so would develop values beneficial to the nation.

In the first half of the nineteenth century, Americans looked to the classical ideas of Pompeii, Rome, and Greece, the Christian symbolism of fourteenth-century Gothic Europe, and the picturesque countryside of fifteenth-century Italy. In the 1850s and 1860s, they admired the appearance of modern Paris and the new buildings of France's Second Empire. In post-Civil War America, the variety of styles, forms, colors, and building materials demonstrated America's vitality, inventiveness, restlessness, and eclectic nature. As the twentieth century began, many Americans longed for the quieter, less hectic eras of the past and preferred versions of the colonial and cottage styles, while others experimented with new house forms. Frank Lloyd Wright, architect of the popular Prairie house, declared, "Democracy needed something basically better than the box."

Americans also studied and borrowed designs in house pattern books. The early books generally included only sketches, floor plans, elevations, or drawings of special architectural components. Individuals who bought the pattern books then took their selected designs to local "carpenter-builders," who supplied the actual working plans and specifications. For much of the nineteenth century, builders, in fact, thought of themselves as architects because they often supplied both the working plans and specifications.

Of all those who published sketches, floor plans, and elevations before the Civil War, none was more influential than Andrew Jackson Downing, a landscape architect. His critical essays about national, social, and moral issues were almost as popular as his designs. Downing, among others, offered specific designs for specific occupations. Stressing that "much of the character of every man may be read in his house," Downing popularized villas, cottages, and farmhouses, all dwellings which he insisted needed to be located on suitable land in the countryside. A villa was "the most refined home of America—the home of its most leisurely and educated class of citizens," and cottages were suitable for "industrious and intelligent mechanics and working men." Farmhouses were to be like farmers—unpretentious, "honest, straightforward and openhearted."

Balloon framing and rail shipment provided cheaper housing and a greater variety of styles. Editors of several periodicals recognized the potential influence of men such as Downing and published their house styles. The perennially popular periodical, *Godey's Lady's Book*, promoted an "own your own home" movement beginning in 1846. For half a century, readers could order drawings for at least 450 different cottage and villa styles. By the end of the century, several magazines, including the widely read *Ladies' Home Journal*, offered readers advice about house styles, furnishings, taste, and manners—important "ingredients for a proper home." Well-known architects and interior decorators contributed designs to the publications. *Ladies' Home Journal* introduced Frank Lloyd Wright to almost a million subscribers. For as little as $5, anyone could order one of Wright's designs.

The carpenter-architects George and Charles Palliser popularized mail-order working specifications. After 1876 they mailed both plans and specifications to clients and prided themselves on their architect-client relationships.

Another nationally known architect of the late nineteenth century, George

Barber of Knoxville, Tennessee, sent building specifications and materials, partial or complete precut house kits, furnaces, fireplaces, mantels, and stained glass by rail. Like the Pallisers, Barber designed most of his houses in a flamboyant Queen Anne Revival style.

The American dream of owning a fashionable home with a well-planned interior became feasible for many families after precut housing became available through mail-order catalogues and when firms such as Sears, Roebuck and Co. provided "mail-order mortgages." Such mail-order designs and house kit catalogues helped spread house styles from Maine to California. Today, these catalogues provide house historians with photographs of actual houses, some original owners' names and addresses, and clues to thinking about the era.

Both house and carriage house were designed by George F. Barber in the Queen Anne Revival style, and all parts and many interior features were shipped by rail to Jeremiah Nunan in Jacksonville, Oregon, in the 1800s. The "American Dream" was as close as the railroad.

Many firms sold precut kits for houses, apartments, churches, schools, and barns. Sears, Roebuck and Co. and Montgomery Ward & Co., however, also offered, as part of an order, everything needed to decorate and furnish a house or apartment. This advertisement is from Sears's 1919 *General Catalog*.

A mail-order shipment could include everything needed to assemble and finish a house. All wooden structural members were precut, numbered, and keyed to the working plans. Some catalogues encouraged buyers to furnish their houses with mail-order purchases and even specified walls where certain pieces fit best. The Aladdin Company of Bay City, Michigan, promised to pay a dollar for every knot found in its lumber. In promoting its "Readi-Cut System," Aladdin pointed to the pyramids, Solomon's Temple, the Washington Monument, and New York's Woolworth Building as structures erected by similar methods. West Virginia's Huntington Lumber and Supply Company, later known as Minter Homes Corporation, offered about a hundred different kits for houses, churches, schools, and garages before 1920. The firm even built whole towns for the United States government. Both Aladdin and Minter shipped house kits overseas, and Minter sold kits through Gimbel's department store in New York. In its 1920 catalogue, Bennett Homes in North Tonawanda, New York, offered the services of interior decorators trained to help "you stock and arrange your kitchen so that you will save time from drudgery of routine, for the enjoyment of a book, the good outdoors, or your social life." Several hundred thousand of these well-built houses, shipped throughout the country in boxes, barrels, crates, and wrappings, still stand. Complete neighborhoods of houses sold by mail-order firms and built by companies for their employees can be found in many areas.

The Great Depression of the 1930s and World War II ended the traditional mail-order housing businesses. After 1945, new types of housing emerged, particularly for suburban housing projects such as the Levittowns in New Jersey and New York and Park Forest in Illinois. Returning GIs needed housing and took advantage of federally guaranteed loans, small down payments, complete prefabricated houses, and the do-it-yourself craze to create new neighborhoods far from city centers.

Transportation and Suburbia

The dramatic growth of rail transportation between 1865 and 1900 made commuting from suburbs to cities a possibility almost everywhere and initiated a major shift in the population. Chicago's suburbs, for example, grew from 50,000 to more than 300,000 during the fifteen years after 1873. As long as commuting was by railroad, and therefore expensive and time-consuming, commuters were almost exclusively wealthy men. Servants, laborers, and gardeners usually did not commute to the neighborhoods in which they worked; instead, they often lived close to the upper-class suburbs.

Intracity commuting initially depended on horse- or mule-drawn vehicles, and their range was limited. The electrification of transportation systems extended the intracity commuting range. Entrepreneurs quickly changed the character of suburbs by establishing streetcar companies in cities across the nation. Oakland and Los Angeles, California, typify the growth patterns created by streetcar owners, who often speculated in land along the streetcar routes. Trolleys or electric streetcars with their nickel-a-ride fares put commuting within the reach of the average wage earner. At the same time, streetcars promoted large scale residential segregation; domestic servants no longer had to live near their employers. Streetcars not only strengthened the practice of segregated communities, they visibly reinforced it on each ride with racially segregated seating.

The popularity of the automobile and the bus brought a new dimension to commuting. Buses, not bound to tracks, could go where commuters lived, and individual automobile ownership provided the ultimate in commuter flexibility. Rail commuting persisted through the early years of the automobile and was sustained by the economic stresses of the 1930s depression and World War II. When the war ended in 1945, a new era of suburbs lay ahead.

Modern Suburbs and Housing Developments

The Levittowns of New York and New Jersey were the largest and most publicized of the early modern suburbs. Abraham Levitt and his sons William and Alfred epitomized the post-World War II suburban developer. Under the pressure of their governmental contract work to build housing for war workers in Norfolk, Virginia, the Levitts developed an assembly-line-like on-site construction method that included the use of as many preassembled components as possible. They revolutionized the residential construction industry to build what Keneneth Jackson calls the biggest private housing project in American history, the original Levittown in Hempstead, New York. Gwendolyn Wright notes that in 1950 the Levitts were "producing one four-room house every sixteen minutes."

Across the country, great numbers of ranch, split-level, and contemporary style houses arose during the 1950s and 1960s; eclectic styles loosely based on traditional designs followed in the 1970s and 1980s. Almost without exception, these houses have attached parking pads or garages, a reflection of what Kenneth Jackson terms the "drive-in society"—a trend that originated in the Southwest and West during the 1920s and 1930s.

Government and Housing

Governments encouraged other changes in the nation's post-1930 residential patterns. In 1933 President Franklin D. Roosevelt initiated the short-lived Home Owners Loan Corporation (HOLC), which provided long-term low-interest mortgages for homes and repair loans. The Federal Housing Authority (FHA), organized in 1934, has continued. The National Housing Act of 1937 (the Wagner-Steagall Act) created the United States Housing Authority (USHA) and authorized it to make loans to local public agencies for slum clearance and housing projects. The law required one unit of public housing to be built for each unit of housing destroyed in slum clearance. The USHA provided the model for post-World War II urban renewal policies. The New Deal also actively promoted "new town" development by financing, building, and managing about a hundred new communities across the country.

By the 1930s, the West End in Cincinnati, Ohio, was a densely settled neighborhood of nineteenth-century two- and three-story buildings. The grid pattern of streets is highlighted in this aerial photograph. The art deco Union Terminal in the upper left corner was completed in the early 1930s. Courtesy of The Cincinnati Historical Society.

By June 1942, the appearance of the West End had changed dramatically. The Cincinnati Metropolitan Housing Authority (CMHA), created in 1933, worked with the Cincinnati Better Housing League and the City Planning Commission to promote decent, safe, and sanitary housing. Their first endeavor was Laurel Homes, the city's first public housing and slum clearance project. The New Deal Public Works Administration provided some of the financing since the project provided construction jobs for about 1,000 local residents. Laurel Homes opened in 1938, with an addition in 1940. Tenants of the 1,039 apartments were selected by social workers. Black and white residents had separate but somewhat equal activities, including clubs, credit unions, a nursery, and newspaper. Later CMHA projects would be racially segregated. Courtesy of The Cincinnati Historical Society.

Governmental influence on housing increased during World War II when the federal government built housing throughout the United States to accommodate military and civilian defense workers at shipyards, military bases, and even college campuses. Entire new communities were built at Hanford, Washington; Oak Ridge, Tennessee; Los Alamos, New Mexico; and Cape Canaveral, Florida; for federal atomic energy projects and, later, the space program.

President Harry S Truman focused on the nation's housing needs, setting as a national goal "a decent home and a suitable living environment for every American family." The National Housing Act of 1949 (NHA) resulted in the destruction of much slum housing with little new public housing built to replace it. Because the new law did not provide for "equivalent elimination," as had the 1937 law, real estate developers could use federal subsi-

Los Alamos, New Mexico

House historians responsible for documenting even a single house in a "company town"—a town that originally had one owner responsible for all housing—or government project can benefit from looking at the town or project's housing as a whole. The general aspects of such housing complexes frequently are well documented. Local newpapers report their advent, graduate students often make them the subject of dissertations and theses in such fields as sociology and business, and government reports may have been issued throughout the government's involvement in a project.

One of the first issues the house historian will want to address for this type of housing is the "why" of the project. Was it a privately sponsored housing project created to fulfill religious or philosophical beliefs? Was the town established around a work site such as a mine or, as in this case study, did the government have a crucial wartime need that could be filled only in a tightly restricted environment?

Knowledge of the "whys" can explain other factors, such as the reasons for the location of the housing and who had responsibility for its design and construction. This case study provides background information on the housing built for U.S. government employees in Los Alamos. It establishes a context for the more than 2,000 housing units— apartments, duplexes, and single family dwellings—that were constructed under government contracts from 1946 to 1962.

After the house historian researched the initial "why, who, and what" of Los Alamos wartime housing in formal histories and other relevant publications, she turned to the issues of post-war housing and ultimate transfer of control to individual private owners. Land records for private ownership are at the Los Alamos County Building, and the Los Alamos Historical Society maintains files on local housing. As the researcher grew up in Los Alamos, she could draw on her personal knowledge of the different groups of houses. She also had a wide variety of contacts to interview for oral histories of "what life was like."

Research for the case study revealed that when the U.S. government possessed the land area now known as Los Alamos, New Mexico, in 1943, the only housing in the remote almost desert-like region were sixteen ranch houses. The isolated area was considered ideal for the installation of a highly secret scientific complex. Even the supplier of the projects' housing, the U.S. Army Corps of Engineers, was subject to

Houses provided to government workers at Los Alamos's Scientific Laboratory between 1946 and 1964 were simply designed and inexpensive to build. This example has a board and batten exterior and might have been built in any inexpensive post-World War II American setting.

strict security measures, and the housing the Corps furnished reflected the urgency of the situation. Los Alamos's wartime housing for the more than 600 families who comprised the scientific community consisted of about 300 buildings, including prefabs, military barracks, Quonset huts, trailers, and dormitories for single men and women.

In 1946, despite the fact that World War II had ended, the government retained total control of Los Alamos's housing, demolished at least part of the "tempos," and constructed approximately 500 permanent residences and 100 prefabricated units. Government contracts to plan the residences were let to W. C. Kruger Company, an architectural engineering firm, and R. E. McKee Company received the construction contracts. The government awarded these two companies a majority of its Los Alamos housing contracts over the next twenty years. Thus, Kruger and McKee played a dominant role in the building of residential Los Alamos.

Throughout the period, they built both multi- and single-family units. Although the names of the groups of single-family houses differed, the amount of space and floor plans were almost identical. A Group 16 three-bedroom house was typical. It was wood frame construction, with wood exterior and sheetrock (drywall) interior. The house had one bathroom and was provided with thermostatically controlled gas-fired forced air heat. The front entry led directly into the living room. On one side were the kitchen and carport. Straight ahead was a hallway which led to the bathroom and bedrooms. An enclosed patio completed the improvements. Housing in Los Alamos was the government version of the tract housing then sweeping the United States.

A statement in 1955 by Norris E. Bradbury, director of the Los Alamos Scientific Laboratory, illustrates some of the problems inherent in this tight governmental control. Bradbury acknowledged that for a long time, the lab has been painfully aware "that the inability of an individual to own his own home is a major cause of concern to residents and major stated cause for termination."

Finally in 1964, the sale of government houses to private individuals began in Los Alamos. The case study's researcher determined that once in the hands of private owners, Los Alamos's housing in general underwent a transition. Almost immediately, homeowners began personalizing their piece of the American dream with additions and remodeling projects.

Case study contributed by Jan Kristin Engel.

---

dies to buy cleared land with no requirement to rebuild housing. Enacted to solve a major national problem—deteriorating inner cities—the NHA had far-reaching negative repercussions, including broken neighborhoods and scattered populations. The 1956 Federal Highway Act further contributed to the destruction of inner-city housing in the path of expressways.

Several of President Lyndon B. Johnson's Great Society programs strengthened the governmental presence in housing. The Housing and Urban Development Act of 1965 created the U.S. Department of Housing and Urban Development (HUD). The Demonstration Cities and Metropolitan Development Act of 1966 included the model cities program to deal with both social and physical aspects of cities and neighborhoods. Although racially restrictive covenants in deeds had been unconstitutional since 1948, the Fair Housing Act of 1968 ended legal racial discrimination in housing and promoted integrated neighborhoods. In 1974 President Richard M. Nixon signed an executive order ending expenditures for public housing. He also discontinued federal support for urban renewal and the model cities programs.

Concerned that urban renewal was destroying too many old buildings, Congress passed the National Historic Preservation Act of 1966 (NHPA). The act made historic preservation an issue in all projects requiring federal permits, licensing, or funding. Beginning in 1976, a series of tax and revenue acts further encouraged historic preservation. The most important of these provided investment tax credits for owners rehabilitating historic properties according to the Secretary of the Interior's *Standards for Rehabilitation and Guidelines for Rehabilitating Historic Buildings*. The guidelines, first promulgated in 1977, became the governing procedures for rehabilitating old buildings if federal funds were involved. For up-to-date information on these acts, contact your State Historic Preservation Office.

Fluctuating interest rates, expensive housing, energy crises, and changes in society and technology have forced Americans since the 1970s to reconsider the ideal home. There are more single parents seeking housing, two wage-earner families, and single adults sharing housing costs. Many desire cost-saving features such as solar heating; others want a return to small backyards or none at all, multiple-use rooms, and housing that can be shared with unrelated owners. Although the dream may still be a new house on its own "smiling lawn," Americans also are buying older houses to renovate, small new houses, log structures, and condominiums. The factory-built mobile and modular house, placed on a grassy plot and given the symbolic trappings of a traditional house, such as decks, picket fences, and porches, more and more is called "home." Today, as for most of the past century, it seems, the dream is coming off the assembly line.

Suggested Readings

Works mentioned or quoted in this chapter are: Aladdin Company, *Aladdin Homes* (Bay City, Mich: Aladdin Co., 1917), p. 7; George F. Barber, *The Cottage Souvenir*, no. 2 (Knoxville: George F. Barber, 1890); George F. Barber, *Modern Dwellings and Their Proper Construction*, 3rd ed. (Knoxville: S. B. Newman & Co., 1901); Ray H. Bennett Lumber Co., Inc., *Bennett Homes: Better Built Ready Cut*, catalogue no. 18 (North Tonawanda, N. Y.: Bennett Homes, 1920), inside back cover; Andrew J. Downing, *The Architecture of Country Houses* 1850 (New York: Dover, 1969); Huntington Lumber and Supply Co., *Minter Homes*, catalogue no. 101 (Huntington, W. Va.: Huntington Lumber and Supply Co., 1916); Sears, Roebuck and Co., *Honor Bilt Modern Homes* (Chicago: Sears, Roebuck and Co., 1924); and Gwendolyn Wright, *Building the Dream: A Social History of Housing in America* (New York: Pantheon Books, 1981), pp. 252-253. The Frank Lloyd Wright quotation is from Virginia and Lee McAlester, *A Field Guide to American Houses* (New York: Knopf, 1984), p. 440; this book is a comprehensive guide to all American house types, including most suburban styles since 1945.

The following publications are also particularly useful for understanding Americans's changing ideas about housing: Wayne Andrews, *Architecture, Ambition, and Americans: A Social History of American Architecture*, rev. ed. (New York: The Free Press, 1978); Catharine Beecher and Harriet Beecher Stowe, *The American Woman's Home* (New York: J. B. Ford, 1869); Clifford Edward Clark, Jr., *The American Family Home, 1800-1960* (Chapel Hill: The University of North Carolina Press, 1986); Jan Cohn, *The Palace or the Poorhouse: The American House as a Cultural Symbol* (East Lansing: Michigan State University Press, 1979); Mary Mix Foley, *The American House* (New York: Harper & Row, 1980); Rolf Goetz, *Rescuing the American Dream: Public Policies and the Crisis in Housing* (New York: Holmes & Meier, 1983); Alan Gowans, *The Comfortable House: North American Suburban Architecture, 1890-1930* (Cambridge: The MIT Press, 1986), which includes a list of companies that built Aladdin mail-order towns for their employees; Alan Gowans, *Images of American Living: Four Centuries of Architecture and Furniture as Cultural Expession* (Philadelphia: Lippincott, 1964); David P. Handlin, *The American Home: Architecture and Society, 1815-1915* (Boston: Little, Brown and Co., 1979); Dolores Hayden, *The Grand Domestic Revolution: A History of Feminist Designs for American Homes, Neighborhoods, and Cities* (Cambridge: The MIT Press, 1981); Dolores Hayden, *Redesiging the American Dream: The Future of Housing, Work, and Family Life* (New York: W. W. Norton & Co., 1984); Colleen McDannell, *The Christian Home in Victorian America, 1840-1900* (Bloomington: Indiana University Press, 1986); Charles W. Moore, Kathryn Smith, and Peter Becker, eds., *Home Sweet Home: American Domestic Vernacular Architecture* (New York: Rizzoli, 1983); Robert A.M. Stern, *Pride of Place: Building the American Dream* (Boston: Houghton Mifflin, and New York: American Heritage Publishing Co., 1986); John R. Stilgoe, "The Suburbs," *American Heritage* 35 (February/March 1984): 20-36; Lindsey Van Gelder, "The Way We Live—Special Ms. Poll: Dream House," *Ms.* 14 (April 1986): 33-36ff; and Gwendolyn Wright, *Moralism and the Modern Home* (Chicago: University of Chicago Press, 1980).

Several publications discuss mail-order housing: Katherine Cole Stevenson and H. Ward Jandl, *Houses by Mail: A Guide to Houses from Sears, Roebuck and Co.* (Washington, D.C.: Preservation Press, 1986); Boris Emmett and John Jeuck, *Catalogues and Counters: A History of Sears, Roebuck and Co.* (Chicago: University of Chicago Press, 1950); James L. Garvin, "The Mail-Order House Plan and American Victorian Architecture," *Winterthur Portfolio* 16 (1981): 309-334; Kay Halpin, "Sears, Roebuck's Best-Kept Secret," *Historic Preservation* 33 (September/October 1981): 24-29; Thomas Harvey, "Mail-Order Architecture in the Twenties," *Landscape* 25 (1981): 1-9; Marylu Terral Jeans, "Restoring a Mail-Order Landmark," *Americana* 9 (May/June 1981): 40-47; Richard Pillsbury, "Farrar Lumber Company, Farrar-Made Houses: A Georgia Product," *Pioneer America* 13 (1981): 49-61; Patricia Poore, "Pattern Book Architecture: Is Yours a Mail-Order House?" *The Old-House Journal* 8 (December 1980): 183, 190-193; and David M. Schwartz, "When Home Sweet Home Was Just a Mailbox Away," *Smithsonian* 16 (November 1985): 90-101. Dolores Fleming, "One Order Brought It All: A Morgantown Mail-Order House," *Goldenseal: West Virginia Traditional Life* 8 (Summer 1982): 36-42, is based on one of the few interviews available with an individual who was the sole owner of a Sears house; this interview is abstracted in Alan Gowans's *The Comfortable House*. House historians could also check with local lumber companies for catalogues of homes designed locally or marketed for a national company. Catalogues from the early twentieth century may be rare, but one may still find house plans advertised at lumber companies today.

For further information on urban development, see John W. Reps, *Town Planning in Frontier America* (Princeton, N.J.: Princeton University Press, 1969); Howard P. Chudacoff, *The Evolution of American Urban Society*, 2nd ed. (Englewood Cliffs, N.J.: Prentice-Hall, 1981); Charles N. Glaab and A. Theodore Brown, *A History of Urban America*, 3rd ed. (New York: Macmillan, 1983); Roy Lubove, ed., *Housing and Planning in the Progressive Era* (Englewood Cliffs, N.J.: Prentice-Hall, 1967); Barbara Rubin, "A Chronology of Architecture in Los Angeles," *Annals of the Association of American Geographers* 67 (1977): 521-537; and Arthur P. Solomon, *Housing the Urban Poor: A Critical Evaluation of Federal Housing Policy* (Cambridge, Mass.: The MIT Press, 1974).

Relevant works on suburbanization include Kenneth T. Jackson, *Crabgrass Frontier: The Suburbanization of the United States* (New York: Oxford University Press, 1985) and Sam Bass Warner, *Streetcar Suburbs: The Process of Growth in Boston, 1870-1900* (Cambridge, Mass.: Harvard University Press, 1962). Both books provide comprehensive bibliographical notes. However, the sampling technique Jackson used does not generate true random samples. *Early Twentieth-Century Suburbs in North Carolina: Essays on History, Architecture and Planning,* edited by Catherine W. Bishir and Lawrence S. Earley (Raleigh: North Carolina Department of Cultural Resources, 1985) reflects the research of individuals involved in understanding the built environment in the context of historic preservation.

In addition to works cited above, other important publications on urbanization include Carl Abbott, *The New Urban America: Growth and Politics in Sunbelt Cities* (Chapel Hill: University of North Carolina, 1981); Blaine Brownell and David Goldfield, eds., *The City in Southern History: The Growth of Urban Civilization in the South* (Port Washington, N.Y.: Kennikat, 1977); John and Laree Caughey, *Los Angeles: Biography of a City* (Berkeley: University of California Press, 1976); Robert M. Fogelson, *The Fragmented Metropolis: Los Angeles, 1850-1930* (Cambridge, Mass.: Harvard University Press, 1967); Theodore Hershberg, *Philadelphia: Work, Space, Family, and Group Experience in the 19th Century: Essays Toward an Interdisciplinary History* (New York: Oxford University Press, 1981); Sherry H. Olson, *Baltimore: The Building of an American City* (Baltimore: The Johns Hopkins University Press, 1980); and Stephan Thernstrom, *The Other Bostonians: Poverty and Progress in the American Metropolis, 1880-1970* (Cambridge, Mass.: Harvard University Press, 1973).

Numerous works published after 1960 focus, at least in part, on the relationship of minorities and immigrants to local housing conditions. Among them are Ronald H. Bayor, *Neighbors in Conflict: The Irish, Germans, Jews, and Italians of New York City, 1929-1941* (Baltimore: The Johns Hopkins University Press, 1978); James Borchert, "Urban Neighborhood Community Informal Group Life, 1850-1970," *Journal of Interdisciplinary History* 11 (Spring 1981): 607-631; and Oliver Zunz, *The Changing Face of Inequality: Urbanization, Industrial Development and Immigrants in Detroit, 1880-1920* (Chicago: University Press of Chicago, 1982).

House historians will find information on government policies at government depositories and libraries. This information has exploded in quantity since the organization of the U.S. Department of Housing and Urban Development in the 1960s, but it is accessible through publications of government documents such as the *Government Publication Monthly Catalog.*

Selected books dealing with government housing issues include John Preston Comer, *New York City Building Control, 1800-1941* (New York: Columbia University Press, 1942); Paul Conkin, *Tomorrow a New World: The New Deal Community Program* (Ithaca: Cornell University Press, 1959); Richard O. Davies, *Housing Reform During the Truman Administration* (Columbia, Mo.: University of Missouri Press, 1966); David E. Dowall, *The Suburban Squeeze: Land Conversion and Regulation in the San Francisco Bay Area* (Berkeley: University of California Press, 1984); James Blaine Hedges, *Building the Canadian West: The Land and Colonization Policies of the Canadian Pacific Railway* (New York: The Macmillan Co., 1939); and Roy Lubove, *The Progressives and the Slums: Tenement House Reform in New York City, 1890-1917* (Pittsburgh: University of Pittsburgh Press, 1962). The American Public Works Association's *History of Public Works in the United States, 1776-1976* (Chicago: American Public Works Association, 1976) includes a chapter on public housing and military installations (including housing), as well as related chapers on sewers and wastewater treatment, solid wastes, and parks and recreation that provide a context for housing development. All the chapters have useful bibliographies for further research. Additional bibliographical material can be found in Suellen M. Hoy and Michael C. Robinson, *Public Works History in the United States: A Guide to the Literature* (Nashville: American Association for State and Local History, 1982).

General books on atomic energy give information on the Oak Ridge, Los Alamos, and Hanford projects. These works include Stephane Groueff, *Manhattan Project: The Untold Story of the Making of the Atomic Bomb* (Boston: Little, Brown and Co., 1967); Anthony Cave Brown and Charles B. MacDonald, *The Secret History of the Atomic Bomb* (New York: Dell Publishing Co., 1977); and Vincent C. Jones, *Manhattan: The Army and the Atomic Bomb* (Washington, D.C.: Government Printing Office, 1985).

To study local private housing reform efforts, check area archives for papers of associations or individuals active in such efforts; these papers may be accompanied by extensive photographic collections. When reviewing newspapers and periodicals, the historian should remember that the reformers, whether organizations or individuals, often publicized the worst possible conditions to prove their point about the need for reform. Historical society journals may also contain pertinent articles.

Relevant periodicals include *Center City Report; Community Development Digest; Historic Preservation; Housing and Development Reporter; HUD Challenge; JAPA: Journal of the American Planning Association; Land Use Digest; Livability; Livability Digest; NAHRO Monitor; Nation's Cities Weekly; Neighborhood: The Journal for City Preservation; Place; Preservation Action Alert; Preservation News;* and *Urban Conservation Report.*

For specific works on historic preservation issues, easements, and historic district legislation as they relate to urban development and government policy toward housing, consult Diane Maddex, ed., *All About Old Buildings: The Whole Preservation Catalog* (Washington D.C.: Preservation Press, 1985). The AASLH Press and the Preservation Press of the National Trust for Historic Preservation publish many books on preservation. For a general overview of historic preservation legislation, see Beth Grosvenor, "Federal Programs in Historic Preservation" in Barbara J. Howe and Emory L. Kemp, eds., *Public History: An Introduction* (Malabar, Fla.: Robert E. Krieger Publishing Co., Inc., 1986).

·7·

The Regional House

HOUSES BUILT WITHOUT FORMAL ARCHITECTURAL DRAW-
ings dot the American and Canadian landscape. These traditional houses,
particularly those built before 1900, often are referred to as folk or vernacular and are clues to the lives of those who settled in an area. While the
English had the greatest influence on housing in the United States and
Canada, people of other nationalities also brought ideas for shelter and
adapted them to local conditions.

Original settlement areas are known as "cultural hearths" or cores. In *Wood,
Brick, and Stone: The North American Settlement Landscape, Volume 1: Houses,*
geographer Allen G. Noble delineates twelve major cultural hearths in North
America. We have focused our discussion on the housing found in several
of these hearths. Within their respective hearths, immigrants constructed
their houses based not only on memories and tradition, but on local materials,
geography, environment, social conditions, and, in varying degrees, on housing standards set by the English in America. Since cultural hearths included
more than one ethnic group, house historians are likely to find more than
one influence on houses in an area.

Settlers moving west carried memories of house types with them. Other
house types remained only where they first appeared. One can follow most
specific house types along the several migratory routes out from the original
hearths. Those that moved the farthest changed the most due to the influence
of other national and local house types, local geographic conditions, and
time. Most early houses have had some stylistic changes and decorative embel-

97

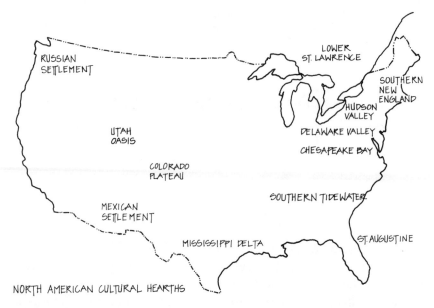

RUSSIAN
SETTLEMENT

LOWER
ST. LAWRENCE

SOUTHERN
NEW
ENGLAND

HUDSON
VALLEY

UTAH
OASIS

DELAWARE VALLEY

CHESAPEAKE BAY

COLORADO
PLATEAU

MEXICAN
SETTLEMENT

SOUTHERN TIDEWATER

ST. AUGUSTINE

MISSISSIPPI DELTA

NORTH AMERICAN CULTURAL HEARTHS

Drawing by Elizabeth Nolin, adapted from Allen G. Noble, *Wood, Brick, & Stone: The North American Settlement Landscape, Vol. 1, Houses.*

lishments. For example, simple houses sometimes became white-columned mansions of Carpenter Gothic cottages.

To identify vernacular housing, the house historian needs to look for alterations while analyzing the shape of the house and its roof; the position of windows and doors, particularly on the front facade; foundations; ornamental details; construction methods and materials; room functions and arrangement, including placement of chimneys; and the house and its site. Generally, America's vernacular houses were greatly influenced by medieval housing in Europe and were characterized by an undisguised use of materials; plain, functional simplicity; and for the most part, nonsymmetrical division of interior and exterior forms and space. Many have had extensions over time, so they have a haphazard added-on appearance. Most are stark but dignified.

House historians might try to answer several questions in order to compare regional housing. Is the house tall and narrow or deep and wide? Is it a one- or two-story house? How many openings are there across the front? How are they arranged? Is there an attached lean-to? What are the shapes and pitches of the various roofs on the house? Is there little ornamentation?

Are windows the casement type or double-hung? How many chimneys are there, and where are they placed? Is there a passage from front to back? Is the house one or two rooms deep? Was the original kitchen location integral to the functions of the family and demands of everyday life? Is the house brick, stone, frame, or log, and how is it constructed?

Take a look at house elements whose design may have been influenced or modified by local conditions such as the availability of one construction material over another, high winds, cold winters and heavy snows, humidity, arid conditions, flooding streams or rivers, insects, or hilly terrain. Several long windows or few small ones; house depth; room alignment; hall, chimney, window, and door placements; steep roof; and height of foundation could reflect adjustments made by builders to the severity of the climate. Sometimes a house type that was considered functional in the core area in one century was too small or poorly arranged in the next, so historians should consider how the same house types changed over time as well.

It is wise to learn which ethnic, religious, and cultural groups first settled in an area. Is there any indication that particular geographical locations such as hilltops or specific house types, sizes, or construction materials were reserved for upper classes or for religious leaders? Some religious communities and plantations had America's first "company housing." Elsewhere, a single house may be all that is left of a larger community that once faced a town square, a country road, a body of water, or the "big house" on the plantation. If the community was Lutheran, house historians might suspect that northern Europeans built the early houses. In the late twentieth century, religion continued to play a dominant role in the architecture of Amish and Mennonite communities.

Because so many vernacular houses are located in rural areas, house historians should be aware that land transportation may have caused a house to "change face" when roads were re-routed because of interstate highways or were built in an area that once depended on river transportation. The present rear facade may once have been the front or vice versa.

The house historian should not assume that all the colonists formed a homogeneous group. Even the English represented different social backgrounds and geographic areas. They brought varied building techniques and memories of houses, making colonial houses in New England very different from those in Virginia. By studying designs and migration patterns for each prototype, historians will begin to understand how the houses in their areas evolved.

The Southern New England cultural hearth. Some of the oldest and best preserved vernacular houses in America are located in southern New England where families from rural southern England settled. Generally, all the colonial vernacular house types in New England can be distinguished by their heavy frame construction, steep roof, massive central chimney, and clapboard wooden siding. There were very few brick or stone houses until the eighteenth century because good clay and lime were not easily available, and settlers were more familiar with heavy framing methods. Few log houses were built in New England even in the earliest settlements.

Within the area, four major house types evolved over two hundred years: the *garrison house,* the *saltbox house,* the *New England large house,* and the *Cape Cod cottage.* (The rare *Rhode Island stone-ender* is not discussed here.) All floor plans revolved around a large central chimney and fireplaces, which provided warmth and heat for cooking. A small winding staircase was located against the chimney within the cramped front entry. Small, asymmetrically placed casement windows, reminiscent of medieval prototypes, were common on seventeenth-century houses.

Only one of the New England house types, the seventeenth-century *garrison house* with its distinctive second-floor overhang, is one room deep. The others are one-and-a-half or two rooms deep, although the second story of the *saltbox house* is only one room deep. The first floor extension on it created kitchen, storage, and bedroom space. By the late seventeenth century, when many New Englanders were building saltbox houses, others were adding lean-tos on the rear of their existing garrison houses, giving them saltbox shapes. Modified garrison houses can be distinguished by the seams that separate the addition.

The largest of the New England types is a full two-story structure—the *New England large house.* A logical extension of the smaller saltbox type, the New England large house contains four to five rooms on each floor. After the balanced facade and paired end chimneys of the Georgian style became popular in the eighteenth century, the traditional New England large house was seldom built. Nevertheless, in time, adaptations of it were influenced by the Greek Revival style and featured the front entrance in a gable end. These adaptations moved into the Mohawk Valley of New York, parts of Michigan, and northern Ohio, all areas to which New Englanders migrated. Another adaptation, the *upright-and-wing house,* includes variations in the location of the front entrance, the chimney, and the size of the wing relative to the main body.

The fourth house type is the one-and-a-half story *Cape Cod cottage,* a house

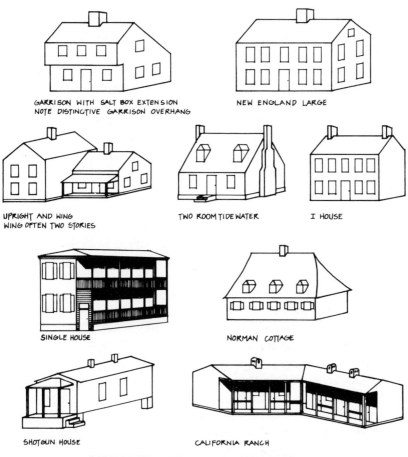

GARRISON WITH SALT BOX EXTENSION
NOTE DISTINCTIVE GARRISON OVERHANG

NEW ENGLAND LARGE

UPRIGHT AND WING
WING OFTEN TWO STORIES

TWO ROOM TIDEWATER

I HOUSE

SINGLE HOUSE

NORMAN COTTAGE

SHOTGUN HOUSE

CALIFORNIA RANCH

SELECTED REGIONAL HOUSING

Drawing by Elizabeth Nolin.

that has distinctive roots in the English countryside. Its steep roof, massive chimney, and ground-hugging shape make it well suited to the windy coasts of New England.

The Chesapeake Bay hearth, sometimes referred to as the *Tidewater hearth,* also was directly influenced by the English, although the Germans and Scotch-Irish had a great impact in areas away from the major Tidewater rivers. Because the region was mostly rural and controlled by large landholders, the cultural hearth was not clearly identifiable. No core city comparable to Boston or Philadelphia influenced settlers. The area's sphere of influence is vast, extending into the Piedmont and Appalachian states, the Carolinas, and Georgia.

The domestic architecture originating in the Chesapeake Bay hearth comprised, at first, framed wood structures. Later, brick construction became common. Prominent features were raised foundations, exterior end chimneys, and a one-room-deep plan. By the eighteenth century, houses were being built with front proches and front-to-rear passages, elements that further aided air circulation—a critical factor in the South. Kitchens were often detached or were part of lean-tos or ells.

Two house types dominated in the Chesapeake Bay cultural hearth. The *hall-and-parlor house,* also called the *two-room Tidewater,* is a one-and-a-half-story dwelling with a relatively steep roof. In time, a distinctive shed-roofed porch and a rear addition with a sloping roof, called a "catslide," became features of the house type. The hall-and-parlor house type did not move far from its cultural core.

The second house type in the Chesapeake Bay hearth, the *I house,* almost always features two rooms stacked over two rooms but has various numbers of bays or facade openings, ranging from two to five across, and various chimney placements. A *Virginia I house* has three bays and often forms the main body of the "grand house" on southern Appalachian plantations. I house types are easy to identify because of their tall height relative to their shallow depth. In contrast, Georgian style grand houses of eastern Virginia plantations have five bays on the front facade but are two rooms deep, while I houses are one room deep. I houses also became important vernacular houses in the Delaware Valley hearth areas, particularly in Pennsylvania.

No matter where it appeared, the I house proved to be popular. The style moved across the Ohio River and beyond; it received its name because of its numbers in Illinois, Indiana, and Iowa, where many, particularly the *five-window I,* still stand. Soon after the I house reached the Midwest, the railroad and extensive building supplies arrived, allowing settlers from the East to build great numbers of them using balloon framing methods.

The Delaware Valley culture area, also known as the *Pennsylvania hearth,* spread out from its Philadelphia core after the late seventeenth century. The diverse ethnic groups in the Delaware Valley moved throughout Delaware, New Jersey, Pennsylvania, northern Maryland and Virginia, the Great Valley of Virginia, and the Appalachian mountains. Swedes, English Quakers,

Finns, Germans, Welsh, and Scotch-Irish built their houses of stone, logs, brick, and frame and also constructed distinctive farmsteads of barns and other buildings. Eventually some of their house types reached the Midwest.

The first New World log structures were built in Delaware and New Jersey in the seventeenth century by Scandinavian and German settlers, who modified the European traditions to meet conditions in the new country. Most log houses have been covered with siding, so house historians often have difficulty recognizing them. Log houses are discussed in more detail in the next chapter.

Although Pennsylvania once had several examples of log and masonry construction (*fachwerk*), German influences are more clearly seen today in Missouri, Wisconsin, Texas, and the Dakotas, where large numbers of Germans settled in the nineteenth century. This German construction system consisted of half timbering with brick or stone nogging. In addition, German housebarns, single structures that housed both people and livestock, are a direct link to Old World building traditions and culture.

Two vernacular house types predominate throughout the Delaware Valley cultural area. *I houses* and large two-room-deep *four-over-four houses* were often constructed of locally quarried stone or local brick. Two-story houses with four rooms over four rooms are distinctive because of their size, which made possible a variety of chimney, window, and door placements. Typically, the two chimneys are built as integral parts of the gable walls, rather than extending out from them. A subtype, the urban rowhouse, had only one chimney. All types were influenced somewhat by the symmetry and flatter roofs of the Georgian and Federal styles.

In the Philadelphia area, English Quakers arriving after 1682 brought memories of the Great London Fire of 1661. Consequently, Philadelphia houses were constructed of brick. They also are more refined than those outside the city.

The Hudson River Valley hearth was settled by the Dutch, Flemish, French Huguenots, English, and Germans. At one time, Dutch influence was pervasive, but now only a few Dutch houses remain. The original Dutch urban houses bore a strong resemblance to city houses in the Netherlands. The Dutch were skillful in building with brick and preferred that material, particularly for urban dwellings. Gables, because of their shapes and locations, were noteworthy features of their houses.

The origins of the extant Dutch rural house types, however, are not so obvious. These houses, reflecting a mix of ethnic influences in the area, are often built of stone with end chimneys, are one-and-a-half stories tall, and have a one-room-deep, elongated floor plan. Straight-edge gables were used earlier than wide projecting eaves and roofs. The Dutch apparently abandoned the custom of connecting their barns to their houses when they arrived in the New World.

The Southern Tidewater hearth. Along the southeastern coast in the Southern Tidewater region, English and Huguenot settlers adapted their houses to the hot climate and urban space. In the summer, families of antebellum South Carolina left their plantations for Charleston because of mosquitoes, malaria, and extreme heat. City land was expensive and, in spite of sea breezes, summers were hot in Charleston. Perhaps contributed by English immigrants from Barbados, one solution to the problems of cost and heat was to alter the traditional placement of the house. When built in urban areas, the house was positioned with its narrow end perpendicular to the street, was raised on stilts to prevent flooding from hurricanes, and lacked one of the side piazzas found on its rural counterpart. Rooms aligned front to back, tall windows and high ceilings, and a second-story verandah or balcony provided much-needed air flow to the urban house. This house type is now known as a *single house* because of its single row of rooms, front to back.

The St. Lawrence Valley hearth. Although the French occupied a substantial amount of land in North America, they did not leave many housing traditions. Fur trappers, traders, and soldiers did not normally bring families and did not need to build permanent homes. Only in a few areas, such as Louisiana; St. Genevieve, Missouri; New Paltz, New York; and French Canada, do houses of French settlers survive. In the lower St. Lawrence Valley of Canada, three important house types bear strong resemblance to houses in western France today.

Located primarily in the area below Quebec City, *Norman cottages* are almost identical to houses in Normandy and resemble some houses in the Mississippi Valley. The Norman cottage is characterized by a steeply pitched roof with hipped ends and bell-cast eaves and was constructed of local fieldstone. The *Quebec cottage* is more widely distributed in the province, and its builders did not rely on one building material or construction method. It, too, has a steep roof but is more massive and medieval in character than the Norman cottage. Although many include a front verandah, which keeps snow away from the front door, its intent was probably more for prestige and fashion. A large stone house, known as the *Montreal house*, has distinctive gables that project above the roof line and create large conspicuous parapets. The gables were evidently safeguards against flames passing from one roof to another in crowded urban conditions, although the surviving houses of this type are found in less populous surroundings. Other early vernacular houses in Canada reflect the adaptation of traditional English cottage styles to the harsh winters and driving winds of the prairies.

Within the Mississippi delta culture area, French elements from Nova Scotia and the French Caribbean islands became mixed with elements from other cultures, particularly black and Spanish. Like houses in Charleston, South Carolina, those in the Mississippi Valley were designed for a hot, humid climate. The predominant house types are one-story with two to four rooms. They were built using the palisade construction (*poteaux-en-terre*) methods and were raised on posts or blocks for air circulation and for protection from water and insects. Some have brick floors that help insulate the houses from the hot air outside and keep dampness to a minimum. A steeply pitched hipped roof is a dominant feature, especially when it extends out over the wide verandahs that often completely encircle the house. Windows and doors are long and narrow, and often each room has a door opening onto the verandah.

The *Louisiana plantation house,* the largest type, is raised on masonry piers almost a full story off the ground. Some of the most luxurious southern mansions reveal the French vernacular building traditions behind classical columns and ornamentation.

The *shotgun house,* which John Vlach attributes to African roots, is usually associated with the South, but its influence spread throughout the country because the style was efficient and inexpensive. It is easily identified because of its narrow gable front, its great length of perhaps three or four rooms, and its doors frequently aligned from front to back, so that one could shoot straight through the house, according to folklore. The name "shotgun," however, probably originated from *to-gan,* a West African word for meeting house.

Great Plains adaptations. In western North America, geography and climate greatly influenced housing, especially where there was little wood. By the late nineteenth century on the Great Plains, pioneers of many backgrounds were building houses of rammed earth. Even though stone was available in some areas of the western plains, it was embedded under layers of soil. An effective solution was to make bricks of sod. An excellent building material, sod insulated the house from the elements and provided good protection from attacks by Native Americans and from severe western storms. Although the pioneers were capable of building rather fashionable two-story sod dwellings with minimal wooden decorative features, most houses were rectangular one-story dwellings with two rooms, few windows, and a single chimney. Some were built partially underground. The sod tradition was supplanted by housing built of milled lumber brought by rail.

Mexican settlement hearth. Much of the southwestern United States and the state of Florida once belonged to Spain and Mexico. Few original colonial houses remain in Florida, but there are several in the southwestern United States. In dry, treeless areas, most houses were constructed of sun-dried adobe bricks or mud-plastered stone until the 1880s when railroad lines brought milled lumber. Thick walls of adobe, stone, and stucco provided excellent insulation. Houses were built room by room, each room being a complete unit with a corner fireplace and shuttered windows. A house could be enlarged by adding another room along one side or around a courtyard. There were often no windows facing the streets.

The *Spanish adobe house* is a long, one-story dwelling with a flat or low pitched roof with projecting logs or poles covered with earth or mud. A courtyard was often an integral part of the living area. Early houses also included a corral with its own courtyard for animals. The *Monterey house* type is also long and usually low. The two-story version often has a balcony. The roof of the Monterey house is generally low-pitched and covered with red tiles.

In California, Spanish and Mexican nobles and soldiers, Yankee merchants, Native American laborers, pioneers, and Forty-Niners influenced housing. However, a gentle climate, plentiful land, and cheap labor meant that a house could spread out with all rooms opening to the outdoors. The ranch house is a well-known descendent of the Spanish house types.

Other vernacular types may be limited to small geographic areas. The Colorado plateau cultural area encompasses Native America housing, and the Utah oasis, housing of the Mormons. Little is known of the Russian settlement area in the northwest, except that it embraced a log tradition. More research needs to be done on housing traditions contributed by blacks, although George McDaniel's *Hearth and Home: Preserving a People's Culture* indicates that blacks did bring to America housing ideas that were used in types of dwellings other than the shotgun house after the Civil War. Obviously, we have not covered all ethnic housing nor all areas of North America. Definitive answers are hard to uncover. In many areas, of course, personal preference, availability of materials, and factors other than ethnicity and geography also influenced vernacular housing.

Suggested Readings

Material for this chapter came partially from the following: Alan Gowans, *Images of American Living: Four Centuries of Architecture and Furniture as Cultural Expression* (Philadelphia: Lippincott, 1964); Peirce Lewis, "Common Houses, Cultural Spoor," *Landscape* 19 (January 1975): 1-22; Virginia and Lee McAlester, *A Field Guide to American Houses* (New York: A. A. Knopf, 1984), important for identifying revival styles; George W. McDaniel, *Hearth and Home: Preserving a People's Culture* (Philadelphia: Temple University Press, 1982); Allen G. Noble, *Wood, Brick, and Stone: The North American Settlement Landscape, Volume 1: Houses* (Amherst: University of Massachusetts Press, 1984); Patricia Poore, "Real Houses, Real Places: 'Vernacular,'" *The Old-House Journal* 14 (April 1986): 106; "Vernacular Houses" series (beginning in February 1986) in *The Old-House Journal*; Richard Pillsbury and Andrew Kardos, *A Field Guide to the Folk Architecture of the Northeastern United States* (Hanover, N.H.: Department of Geography, Dartmouth [College], 1970); Richard Pillsbury, "Patterns in the Folk and Vernacular House Forms of the Pennsylvania Culture Region," *Pioneer America* 9 (July 1977): 13-29; William Tishler, "German Immigrants Brought Old World to Midwest," *Preservation News* 26 (October 1986): 12-13; and John M. Vlach, "The Shotgun House: An African Architectural Legacy" in *Common Places: Readings in American Vernacular Architecture*, edited by Dell Upton and John M. Vlach (Athens: University of Georgia, 1986).

A major bibilography on vernacular architecture is Howard Wight Marshall, *American Folk Architecture: A Selected Bibliography* (Washington, D.C.: American Folklife Center, Library of Congress, 1981). Information about regional housing includes Mac E. Barrick, "The Log House as Cultural Symbol," *Material Culture* 18 (1986): 1-19; Henry Glassie, *Patterns in the Material Folk Culture of the Eastern United States* (Philadelphia: University of Pennsylvania Press, 1971); Fred Kniffen, "Folk Housing: Key to Diffusion," *Annals of the Association of American Geographers* 55 (1965): 549-577; Allen G. Noble, *Houses*, noted above, and his Volume 2, *Barns and Farm Structures* (Amherst: University of Massachusetts Press, 1984); John R. Stilgoe, *Common Landscape of America, 1580-1845* (New Haven: Yale University Press, 1982); *Sunset Magazine* and Cliff May, collaborator, *Sunset Western Ranch Houses*, 3rd printing (San Francisco: Lane Publishing Co., Inc., 1950); and Dell Upton, ed., *Architectural Roots: Ethnic Groups that Built America* (Washington, D. C.: Preservation Press, forthcoming). Essays treating American vernacular architecture from rural black communities in Ohio to housing in Newfoundland are found in Dell Upton and John M. Vlach, eds., *Common Places: Readings in American Vernacular Architecture* (Athens: University of Georgia, 1986); Camille Wells, ed., *Perspectives in Vernacular Architecture* (Annapolis: Vernacular Architecture Forum, 1982); and Camille Wells, ed., *Perspectives in Vernacular Architecture II* (Columbia: University of Missouri Press, 1986). For information about recent publications documenting the Chinese in Hawaii, write the University of Hawaii Press, Honolulu, Hawaii.

Other pertinent publications include the following: Mary Mix Foley, *The American House* (New York: Harper & Row, 1980); Herbert Gottfried and Jan Jennings, *American Vernacular Design, 1870-1940: An Illustrated Glossary* (New York: Van Nostrand, 1985); Michael Hurewitz, "Built to Last: New York State's Extraordinary Stone Houses are Monuments to Dutch and Huguenot Craftsmanship," *Historic Preservation* 38 (July/August 1986): 49-53; Thomas C. Hubka, *Big House, Little House, Back House, Barn: The Connected Farm Buildings of New England* (Hanover, N.H.: University Press of New England, 1984); Terry G. Jordan, *American Log Buildings* (Chapel Hill: University of North Carolina Press, 1985); Charles E. Martin, *Hollybush: Folk Building and Social Change in an Appalachian Community* (Knoxville: University of Tennessee, 1984); Thomas J. Schlereth, "Historic Houses as Learning Laboratories: Seven Teaching Strategies," American Association for State and Local History Technical Leaflet 105, *History News* 33:4 (April 1978); and Marcus Whiffen and Frederick Koeper, *American Architecture, 1607-1976* (Cambridge, Mass.: The MIT Press, 1981).

Relevant periodicals include *Association of American Geographers Annals; Geographical Review; Historic Preservation; Journal of Architectural Education; Journal of Cultural Geography; Journal of American Culture; Journal of Interdisciplinary History; Journal of the Society of Architectural Historians; Landscape; Material Culture* (formerly *Pioneer America: The Journal of Historic American Material Culture); Sunset Magazine; The Old-House Journal;* and *Winterthur Portfolio: A Journal of American Material Culture.* The newsletters of the Pioneer America Society, the Vernacular Architecture Forum, and the Society of Architectural Historians also include book reviews, bibliographies, and information about traditional vernacular housing. See also publications by State Historic Preservation Offices, local and statewide history or historic preservation organizations, and the sources cited in chapter 2.

·8·

Construction Techniques and Materials

NORTH AMERICAN TECHNIQUES OF HOUSE CONSTRUC-
tion, with the exception of those used in buildings of more than two stories, have composed a craft tradition that remains in the hands of local
builders and trained architects. With few exceptions this tradition was brought
from Europe and adapted to American conditions. A building's structural
system and materials can provide valuable clues to the date of construction
and, as noted in the previous chapter, to the cultural background of its builder
or first occupants.

Heavy Timber Construction Techniques

The post and beam (or trabeated) construction system is of ancient origin
and has been used for houses, barns, mills, and factories. The best known
post and beam construction is the half-timbered house in which spaces
between the timbers are filled with brick, wattle and daub, or even cord
wood. These infilling materials could be covered with stucco, or the entire
structure could be covered with wood siding. This type of house construction is usually associated with the colonial period, but it also was used later.
For example, German settlers in Old Salem, North Carolina, and Bethle-
hem, Pennsylvania, employed it extensively. This construction technique
later spread to the Midwest as Germans migrated there in the nineteenth
century.

Another common heavy timber system is log house construction, which
uses handhewn timbers or notched logs. The traditional log house had logs
arranged horizontally, one on top of the other. However, in Quebec and

Louisiana, the French introduced palisade construction, called *poteaux-en-terre*, consisting of heavy vertical posts driven into the ground close together. Like half-timber construction and horizontal log construction, the spaces between posts were filled with nogging. This technique was used to build army stockades as well as houses. Because the logs tended to rot in the ground, the system was improved by building a field stone foundation, installing a timber sill plate on top of the foundation, setting the logs on it, and installing a plate on top of the posts.

Log structures can be linked to specific immigrant groups by examining the type of notching used. For example, for the wet winters in the eastern United States, the German dovetail notches are far superior to the half-notch. Equally important, they are much more rigid because the logs are locked together.

Although large strong timbers were used, the log wall was not very stable unless supported by closely spaced cross or end walls. Door and window openings cut into the logs decreased the strength of the walls. Thus, rooms in log houses are usually small with walls not longer than eighteen to twenty feet.

House historians can find clues to the methods employed to prepare trees for use as structural members by looking for ax marks on heavy timber beams or various types of saw marks on smaller beams and joists. The simplest technique was to remove the bark and notch the logs to receive other logs. In some cases, post and beam timbers were too heavy or large in diameter to use "in the round." Then, tree trunks were hewn into square or rectangular members, leaving clearly visible ax marks on the timbers. In addition, the ends of the logs were usually "squared off," exposing a pattern of growth rings at the ends.

In heavy timber construction wooden pegs were used throughout the nineteenth century. The pegs or treenails (pronounced "trunnels") were driven into bored holes to lock the timber joints together. Later in the century, iron and steel bolts replaced the treenail altogether.

Although we cherish log cabins and see them as symbolic of our frontier heritage, our ancestors considered them temporary and utilitarian at best. Owners of more permanent log houses often added wood siding or brick on the exterior and plaster on the interior—materials that completely covered the hewn timber construction. The exterior covering also protected the logs from the weather. Similarly, many post-and-beam frame buildings were covered

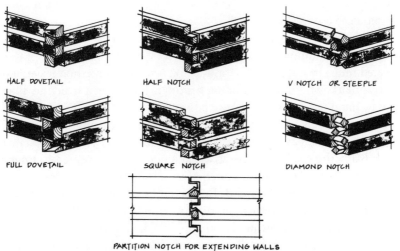

HALF DOVETAIL

HALF NOTCH

V NOTCH OR STEEPLE

FULL DOVETAIL

SQUARE NOTCH

DIAMOND NOTCH

PARTITION NOTCH FOR EXTENDING WALLS

NOTCHING SYSTEMS USED IN LOG CONSTRUCTION

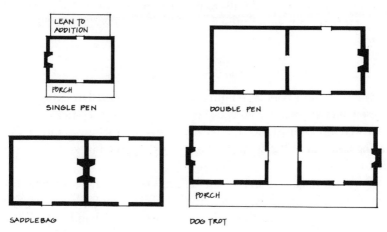

LEAN TO ADDITION

PORCH

SINGLE PEN

DOUBLE PEN

SADDLEBAG

PORCH

DOG TROT

BASIC LOG HOUSE FORMS

Drawing by Elizabeth Nolin.

with wood, Insulbrick® or Brick Tex,® or aluminum siding. Wall thickness and roof framing provide evidence of a log structure hidden behind the protective covering.

Wood building components can be prepared in a variety of ways. The wood used in house framing may have been sawn by hand, by sash saws of water-powered mills, by circular saws, or by band saws. Each method leaves a distinctive mark, which will aid house historians in dating a structure. Planks sawn by hand out of large logs have rather widely spaced vertical saw marks. Early water-powered sash mills produced lumber with similar vertical saw marks. Unless the house predates the nineteenth century, any vertical marks are probably the result of a sash saw. The circular saw, invented in England in 1814 but not used in North America until the 1840s, left distinctive crescent shaped marks on the wood. By the 1880s, giant band saws similar to those still used in modern lumber mills, were in operation. Band saws made closely spaced vertical saw marks on lumber. These vertical marks are quite different from those left by the early sash saws. Much of the lumber prepared in band saw mills was planed to produce standard lumber sizes. Scroll saws and jig saws allowed mills to produce the elaborate "gingerbread" seen on Victorian era houses in the form of brackets, bargeboards, balusters, and lintels.

Balloon Framing Techniques

By far the most popular framing system was invented in Chicago in 1833. It used lumber sawn to standard sizes in relatively small "sticks," called *studs*, that were uniformly spaced, typically at sixteen inches, to form a light yet strong and stiff wall system. Because of its supposed lack of solidity, it was derisively called "balloon" framing.

The many nails used in balloon framing are another way to date construction, additions, or repairs. Before the Civil War, cut nails produced by special machines replaced the earlier, more expensive hand made nails. Cut nails were sheared or cut in a tapered shape from iron and later from steel plates. Next, a machine formed a head on the nail by cold forging. Later in the nineteenth century, wire nails were produced in huge quantities and in a large variety of sizes and shapes for construction and other applications. Sawn lumber from Douglas fir and redwood trees, plus the availability of sixty-five thousand wire nails per house, inspired builders to construct the five-room California (or San Francisco) stick style house with its elaborate woodwork.

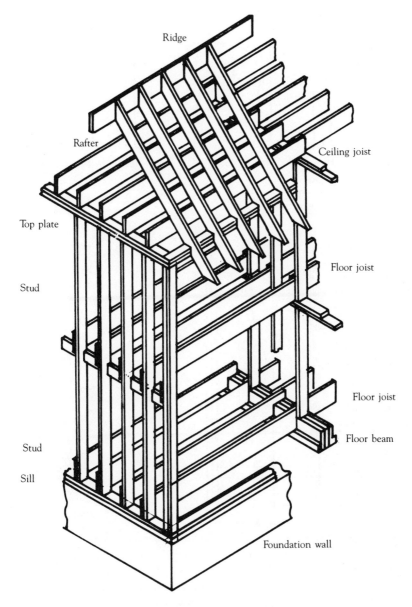

Ridge

Rafter

Ceiling joist

Top plate

Floor joist

Stud

Floor joist

Stud

Floor beam

Sill

Foundation wall

This illustration of the balloon-frame construction system shows how precut, standard size pieces of lumber could be nailed together to produce a sturdy house. Drawing by Emory L. Kemp.

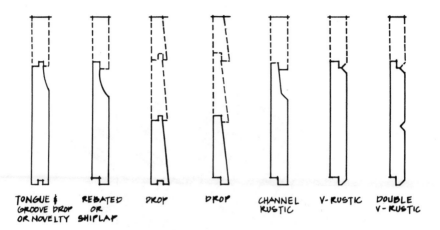

TONGUE & GROOVE DROP OR NOVELTY   REBATED OR SHIPLAP   DROP   DROP   CHANNEL RUSTIC   V-RUSTIC   DOUBLE V-RUSTIC

TYPES OF SIDING

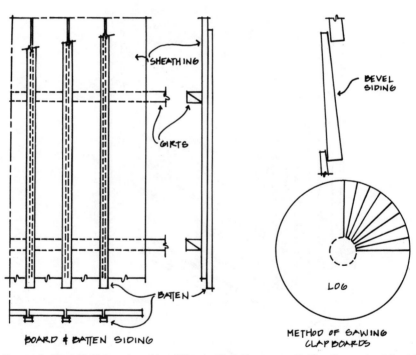

SHEATHING

GIRTS

BATTEN

BOARD & BATTEN SIDING

BEVEL SIDING

LOG

METHOD OF SAWING CLAPBOARDS

Drawing by Elizabeth Nolin, adapted from Whitney Clark Huntington, *Building Construction: Materials and Types of Construction,* © 1982, John Wiley & Sons.

House historians who want to describe the exterior of a historic wood house will need to examine the building's siding. As illustrated, the siding may be joined in a variety of ways—tongue and groove, drop, shiplap, rustic, bevel, or board and batten. Hand riven (split) shiplap siding could date back to the eighteenth century, and board and batten is popularly associated with the Gothic Revival style of the mid-nineteenth century. However, there are no set rules that correlate the type of siding with the date of a house. Saw marks and nail types are far more reliable indicators of the period in which a home was erected.

Metal Construction Techniques

The introduction of iron and steel as building materials in the nineteenth century produced a wide range of new building forms. While houses could be built of wood, large, multistory apartment houses needed iron or steel framing systems to provide open and flexible space, height, and fire protection. In America, steel, the successor and near relative of wrought iron, was most often used in the skyscraper, which arose out of the ashes of the 1871 Chicago fire to become one of the great American contributions to the building arts.

The widespread use of iron and, later, steel by engineers transformed the craft tradition in building to one based on engineering principles and firmly rooted in the science of mechanics and mathematics. Equally important, the application of iron and steel to buildings also brought about the schism of architecture and civil engineering into separate professions.

Iron and steel have not substituted for wood in small structures because they are much more expensive and cannot be fitted or cut to length on site. Still, iron and steel beams and columns often replace large timber summer (a corruption of the French *sommier* meaning "girder") beams, which became increasingly difficult and expensive to obtain. Iron and steel beams in basements were supported on cast iron and later steel columns. While iron and steel members have found limited structural use in house construction, both materials have been widely used since the 1840s in corrugated and standing seam roofs, which are popular because they are light in weight, weathertight, and inexpensive.

Iron was used in prefabricated buildings, including houses, churches, and schools, and in components for buildings, such as cast iron facades or beams, before the mid-nineteenth century. Prefabricated metal structures are sel-

dom associated with housing, with two notable exceptions: the Lustron®
Home and the mobile home. Developed shortly after World War II, the
Lustron® Home had a steel skin with a baked-on protective porcelain coat-
ing, which required no painting. The entire house was framed in steel. The
Lustron® Corporation became insolvent after a few years and production
ceased. Thereafter, the prefabricated house remained firmly in the hands
of those using wooden materials and traditional approaches to house construction. The metal prefabricated house of today consists almost exclusively
of the mobile home, an outgrowth of the factory-produced travel trailer. While
some attempts have been made recently to use plastics in prefabricated houses,
this market has been limited.

The most prevalent use of metal in vernacular housing has been exterior
metal siding. Thin sheets of iron or steel are pressed and painted to imitate
fine stonework or other materials. A similar technique is used to replicate
elaborate plaster work, especially for ceilings. These pressed metal products,
available in sheets or coils, were simply nailed to the surface and then painted.
Pressed metal products became available in the mid-nineteenth century and
were advertised in catalogues distributed by manufacturers around the country.
House historians may find these catalogues in libraries or may locate advertisements for the products in newspapers. Each company had unique patterns, so it may be possible to match a catalogue ad with a ceiling in place
in a house. However, because the light-weight products were easy to ship,

This home in Morgantown, West Virginia, shows the steel paneled exterior typical of homes built
by the Lustron® Company.

some manufacturers had nationwide distribution systems. The popular aluminum siding widely used in the late twentieth century is a direct descendent of these earlier pressed metal products.

Masonry Materials

In North America bricks, stones, terra cotta units, adobe, and concrete blocks are the most popular masonry materials. Masonry units are produced in small blocks and are used with some type of cement-like material (mortar) in order to produce a large building element such as a wall. The individual masonry units are strong in compression (load bearing) but weak in tension (stretching action). Masonry, therefore, can be employed successfully in structural elements subjected to direct compressive loads—load bearing walls, piers, and columns. Masonry can be used to span openings only if it is formed into arches, vaults, and domes.

Brickwork was used thousands of years before the Christian era. After long neglect, brick became a popular building material in Britain in the sixteenth century. English colonists in North America used brick for churches and public buildings as well as for the houses of the well-to-do. German immigrants used it extensively in their communities, both rural and urban.

The production method and the clay material used in brick-making can provide information valuable to house historians. By identifying the clay used and the method of firing, the researcher often can date the brick and locate the source of production.

For centuries, brick has been made by the soft-mud process wherein clay is mixed with water and worked into a uniform, mudlike (or plastic) mass. This mixture then is pressed by hand into molds. By the mid-nineteenth century, machines were developed to press the pliable clay into bricks.

Other methods of brick-making introduced in the nineteenth century are now standard procedures. In the stiff-mud process of brick-making, just enough water is added to the clay to make the mixture thin enough to be extruded through a die in a long continuous ribbon, rather like toothpaste squeezed from a tube. Brick is then made by cutting the ribbon with a taut wire, producing "wire-cut" brick. Brick can also be made by the dry-pressed method in which compacted dry clay is pressed into gang-molds. These bricks are the most uniform in dimension since they shrink very little during firing.

The strength, durability, and uniformity of bricks depend on the temperature at which they are fired and the type of clay used. In many cases, pre-Civil War bricks were fired on-site in crudely built ovens. Bricks were fired from the center by covering stacks of green bricks and wood with a mound of sod in which openings were left at both the top and the bottom. The wood was ignited, and the bricks were fired from the heat produced. Those bricks nearest the center were fired at a higher temperature than those on the periphery. Thus, this method produced soft burnt bricks that varied widely in color and strength because of the difference in temperature from one part of the mound to another. These bricks are not durable and often are protected by paint or stucco. Thus, proper preservation treatment for soft brick structures includes repainting or restuccoing to avoid exposing the bare bricks to weathering.

A considerable improvement came with the introduction of the beehive brick kiln. In this process, green bricks were stacked inside the kiln and then fired from the kiln's center. Because the kiln could not be uniformly heated, the bricks in the center were fired at a higher temperature than those along the outside walls. Bricks fired in a beehive kiln vary in color and strength, with the harder brick being a darker color than the others. Modern bricks are fired in a continuous kiln in which every brick passes through at the same temperature and for the same length of time to produce a uniform product.

To be used in house construction, bricks have to be bonded together. Lime mortar, consisting of lime and sand, is the traditional bonding material. Because lime is somewhat soluble in water, lime mortar cannot be used below ground or in a damp environment. For vertical surfaces with carefully struck joints, lime mortar produces durable walls that rarely need to be repointed. Lime mortar is white in color and is so soft that it can be scratched with a fingernail. It is relatively elastic and will absorb a considerable amount of movement in a wall or pier before it loses its bond to the brick. Apart from its lack of long-term durability, it is an ideal mortar.

For a more durable, waterproof mortar, natural cement and, later, Portland cement were used instead of lime. The resulting mortar is much stronger and far less elastic. Natural cement mortar is typically tan in color; Portland cement mortar is usually grey. Within a locality, various cement materials were used as mortars during specific periods. By 1905, Portland cement was being used on a national scale. Therefore, the type of mortar used can lead to conclusions about the date of construction. If specific analysis is necessary, consult the State Historic Preservation Office for guidelines.

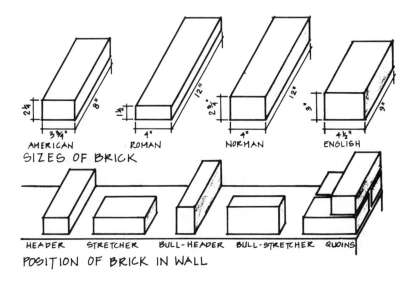

SIZES OF BRICK

2¼" / 8" / 3¾"	1½" / 12" / 4"	2¾" / 12" / 4"	3" / 9" / 4½"
AMERICAN	ROMAN	NORMAN	ENGLISH

HEADER   STRETCHER   BULL-HEADER   BULL-STRETCHER   QUOINS

POSITION OF BRICK IN WALL

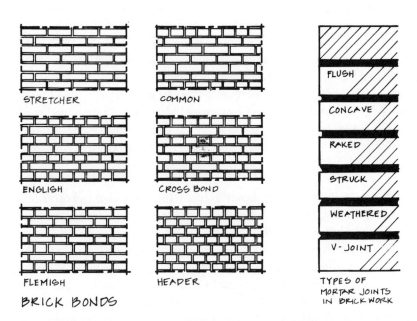

STRETCHER

COMMON

ENGLISH

CROSS BOND

FLEMISH

HEADER

BRICK BONDS

FLUSH

CONCAVE

RAKED

STRUCK

WEATHERED

V-JOINT

TYPES OF
MORTAR JOINTS
IN BRICKWORK

Drawing by Elizabeth Nolin, adapted from Whitney Clark Huntington, *Building Construction: Materials and Types of Construction,* © 1982, John Wiley & Sons.

The pattern of laying up the brickwork varies depending on whether the building is constructed with one or two layers of brick. For buildings with more than one layer, a brick, or "header," is placed perpendicular to the wall surface so that only its end shows. The header ties together the separate layers. Over the centuries, many brick bonding patterns have been developed to provide strong, economical, and attractive walls and other surfaces. The most popular structural bond is called "gardenwall," "common," or "American" bond, with five or six stretcher courses of brickwork followed by a header course. Stretcher bond is also widely used in brickwork that is only one brick thick and not expected to be load bearing.

Identifying the pattern used on a brick structure is an important part of describing the exterior of the building. All of the brick patterns used in the United States were developed in Europe before the colonists settled the New World; therefore, it is not possible to assign dates to particular brick patterns as one assigns dates to architectural styles. While patterns do tend to get simpler over time, from the Flemish bond used in the colonial period to the stretcher bond used today, this is in large part due to changing construction techniques. Balloon frame or metal frame buildings carry the weight of the building on the frame, so the brick is used simply as a veneer. In that case, headers in the wall may be false, or simply half bricks, instead of true headers tying together the two walls of the brick house.

As a building material clay is usually thought of in terms of fired bricks. However, it was and is employed as sun-dried bricks, cob, rammed earth, and adobe in many parts of the world. Much adobe construction is located in the desert Southwest of the United States and is associated with the Hispanic and Native American cultures of that region.

Terra cotta in the form of hollow tile block has been used in both houses and large buildings since the late nineteenth century in America. In houses, it was used for basement walls, occasionally for interior partition walls that were finished with plaster, and for exterior walls that were usually finished with stucco. Hollow tiles were also used widely as an inexpensive backing material for both brick and stone walls. Different sizes and shapes of tiles have been produced, including inexpensive mass-produced architectural terra cotta, for exposed surfaces. The use of terra cotta for cornices and decorative detailing provided great freedom of ornamentation. The most visible and widely known use of terra cotta is for roof tiles. These products are illustrated in manufacturers' catalogues and may be used in dating a house.

In Terlingua, Texas, this adobe school was built to serve a mercury mining town. Of the many adobe structures in the community, this is the best preserved.

Concrete blocks. About the same time clay tiles were becoming popular, hollow concrete blocks were used for both foundations and walls. Historically, when new materials were introduced in the building industry, they first imitated an already accepted product. Concrete blocks, for example, were formed to look like stone and were used in constructing whole houses in the first three decades of the twentieth century. Today, concrete blocks are being used for party walls, small scale commerical buildings, and walls to be surfaced with brick veneer and stucco.

Concrete reinforced with steel was first used in America in the Ward House in the 1870s in Westchester County, New York. Despite the great popularity of reinforced concrete today, its use in houses has been restricted largely to foundations and to slabs on grade for houses without basements. Town houses and apartment buildings of the 1960s to 1980s also used precast concrete for slab floors and walls, which could be cast with decorative patterns on the exposed surface. Precast concrete provides an economical and fireproof construction and is widely used in the West.

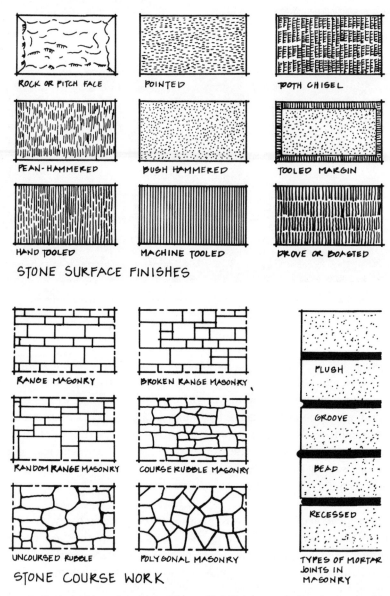

ROCK OR PITCH FACE   POINTED   TOOTH CHISEL

PEAN-HAMMERED   BUSH HAMMERED   TOOLED MARGIN

HAND TOOLED   MACHINE TOOLED   DROVE OR BOASTED

STONE SURFACE FINISHES

RANGE MASONRY   BROKEN RANGE MASONRY

RANDOM RANGE MASONRY   COURSE RUBBLE MASONRY

UNCOURSED RUBBLE   POLYGONAL MASONRY

STONE COURSE WORK

FLUSH

GROOVE

BEAD

RECESSED

TYPES OF MORTAR
JOINTS IN
MASONRY

Drawing by Elizabeth Nolin, adapted from Whitney Clark Huntington, *Building Construction: Materials and Types of Construction,* © 1982, John Wiley & Sons.

Stone. Like wood siding and brick patterns, stone types, patterns, and finishes can add to the description of the exterior of a building. Long-time residents may know the location of former quarries that supplied local building materials, the type of stone found in the quarries, and the dates the quarries operated. If stone is hand-chiseled, uneven chisel marks can be found on the blocks. But stone masonry patterns, like their brick counterparts, are not usually a reliable means of dating a house.

Like bricks and other clay products, stone blocks are bonded together with mortar. Unlike brick, however, stone work is occasionally laid up dry, without mortar, although this is rare in the case of North American dwellings. The cost of stone construction varies greatly from the most expensive type of masonry using fine ashlar to what is perhaps the cheapest form of building, namely rubble masonry composed of field stones and lime mortar made on the site by firing limestone.

Trim stone is widely used in brick and stone houses for belt courses, quoins, sills, lintels, and jambs. Stone is also used in the interior of houses for mantels, hearths, floors, steps, and stairways. Field stone was the standard foundation material for houses before the introduction of concrete blocks.

Glass

The availability of glass in various sizes has had a profound influence on architectural design. Over the years, the size of window panes that could be manufactured dictated the type of windows builders used in houses. In the case of colonial buildings, the window had to be divided into a series of "lites" that accommodated the small hand-blown panes then available. Double-hung windows in colonial times could have as many as twelve lites or panes per sash. Through the nineteenth century, the number of panes was reduced to one or two per sash as the technology was developed to manufacture larger sheets of glass.

The traditional hand-blown crown glass pane was produced by skilled glass blowers in a series of steps. First, a large globe of molten glass was attached to the end of an iron rod. This hollow sphere was spun into a flat disk with the rod attached at the center, leaving a distinctive bull's-eye or crown in the middle of the pane. The diameter of the disks was determined by the amount of air the blower could deliver into the blow-pipe. Rectangular panes were then cut from the disk.

In the 1830s the hand-blown cylinder process was introduced to England from France. This involved elongating a globe of molten glass into a cylinder by swinging it in a pit. The cylinder then had its ends removed and was slit longitudinally so that it could be opened up to produce a flat sheet. Much larger sheets could be produced by this method, but the glass blower's air supply still set limits. Both crown and cylinder glass can be distinguished from machine-made glass by imperfections such as air bubbles, variations in thickness, and "feathers" or lines in the glass.

By mid-century, specially designed machines manufactured sheet and plate glass, eliminating hand blowing. These machines were capable of producing much larger sheets in great quantities to meet the demands of rapidly growing industrial cities.

The Art Deco style of architecture, popular in the 1920s, featured glass blocks that could be laid up like masonry units to form opaque walls. Glass blocks have made a modest reappearance in a few contemporary houses and apartment buildings.

While original glass in a building can provide a rough method of dating the building, glass is also the most fragile building material and may not survive as original building components. Windows may well be broken and replaced over the years, so that one finds modern glass in a nine-lite window in a nineteenth-century house. Original glass is most likely to survive in out-of-the-way windows, such as those in the gable.

Understanding the materials and construction techniques used in a building can lead the researcher to insights into the history of a particular house. It also can lead to an appreciation of the skills and aesthetic sensibilities of the craftspeople who constructed the house.

Suggested Readings

The following books provide a general introduction to building construction, particularly as it relates to homes: Chesley Ayers, *Specifications: For Architecture, Engineering, and Construction*, 2nd ed. (New York: McGraw-Hill Book Co., 1984); Francis D. K. Ching, *Building Construction Illustrated* (New York: Van Nostrand Reinhold, 1975); Albert G. H. Dietz, *Dwelling House Construction*, 4th ed., rev. (Cambridge, Mass.: The MIT Press, 1974); Whitney Clark Huntington, *Building Construction: Materials and Types of Construction*, 5th ed. (New York: John Wiley & Sons, 1982); Virginia and Lee McAlester, *A Field Guide to American Homes* (New York: Alfred A. Knopf, 1984); Joseph G. McNeill, *Principles of Home Inspection: A Guide to Residential Construction, Inspection and Maintenance* (New York: Van Nostrand Reinhold Co., 1979); Charles E. Peterson, ed., *Building Early America: Contributions Toward the History of a Great Industry; The Carpenters' Company of the City and County of Philadelphia* (Radnor, Pa.: Chilton Book Co., 1976); William A. Radford, *Old House Meas-*

ured and Scaled Detail Drawing: An Early Twentieth Century Pictorial Sourcebook (New York: Dover Publications, Inc., 1983); Ronald C. Smith, *Principles and Practices of Light Construction,* 3rd ed. (Englewood Cliffs, N.J.: Prentice-Hall, Inc., 1980); and Ronald C. Smith, *Materials of Construction,* 2nd ed. (New York: McGraw Hill, 1973). See also Michael J. Doucet and John C. Weaver, "Material Culture and the North American House: The Era of the Common Man, 1870-1920," *Journal of American History* 72 (March 1985): 560-587.

A guide to reading construction blueprints is Mark W. Huth, *Basic Construction Blueprint Reading* (New York: Van Nostrand Reinhold Co., 1980).

Books on specialized building materials include: H. Ward Jandl, ed., *The Technology of Historic American Buildings: Studies of the Materials, Craft Processes, and the Mechanization of Building Construction* (Washington, D.C.: Foundation for Preservation Technology for the Association for Preservation Technology, 1983) and Harley J. McKee, *Introduction to Early American Masonry: Stone, Brick, Mortar & Plaster* (Washington, D.C.: Preservation Press, 1973). Books that describe the various techniques of glass-making include: Harlan Logan, ed., *How Much Do You Know about Glass?* (New York: Dodd, Mead & Company, 1951); F.J. Terence Maloney, *Glass in the Modern World: A Study of Materials Development* (Garden City, N.Y.: Doubleday Science Series, Doubleday & Company, Inc., 1968); Rune Persson, *Flat Glass Technology* (New York: Plenum Press, 1969); and Frances Rogers and Alice Beard, *5,000 Years of Glass* (New York: Frederick A. Stokes Company, 1937).

Books on specialized types of house construction include: Donna Ahrens, Tom Ellison, and Ray Sterling, *Earth Sheltered Homes: Plans and Designs* (New York: Van Nostrand Reinhold Co., 1981); Carl and Barbara Giles, *Steel Homes* (Blue Ridge Summit, Pa.: Tab Books, Inc., 1984); Robert L. Roy, *Underground Houses: How to Build a Low-Cost Home* (New York: Sterling Publishing Co., 1979); and Paul Graham McHenry, *Adobe and Rammed Earth Buildings: Design and Construction* (New York: John Wiley & Sons, 1984). Although probably not widely available, Carlton M. Edwards, *Homes for Travel and Living: The History of the Recreation Vehicle and Mobile Home Industries* (East Lansing, Mich.: Carl Edwards and Associates, 1977) is an excellent history of mobile homes, from camping trailers to the modern mobile home business; it also discusses the development of facilities to serve mobile homes from primitive campgrounds to modern mobile home parks. For further information on prefabricated buildings in the nineteenth century, see Gilbert Herbert, *Pioneers of Prefabrication: The British Contribution in the Nineteenth Century* (Baltimore: The Johns Hopkins University Press, 1978). For illustrations and brief descriptions of framing systems, see "Traditional House Framing" in *The Old-House Journal* 8 (December 1980): 197-199.

Books that help historians in dating, identifying regional types, and restoring log buildings include: James Fitch, *American Building: The Historical Forces that Shaped It* (New York: Schocken Books, 1965); Harrison Goodall and Renee Friedman, *Log Structures: Preservation and Problem-Solving* (Nashville: American Association for State and Local History, 1980); Henry Glassie, *Folk Housing in Middle Virginia: Structural Analysis of Historical Artifacts* (Knoxville: University of Tennessee Press, 1975); Henry Mercer, *The Origin of Log Cabins* (Doylestown, Pa.: Bucks County Historical Society, 1926); and Hugh Morrison, *Early American Architecture* (New York: Oxford University Press, 1952).

Books on the adaptive reuse of buildings include: Ernest Burden, *Living Barns: How to Find and Restore a Barn of Your Own* (New York: Bonanza Books, 1977) and Elisabeth Kendall Thompson, *Recycling Buildings: Renovations, Remodelings, Restorations, Reuses* (New York: McGraw-Hill Book Co., 1977).

The *Preservation Briefs* series available from State Historic Preservation Offices includes short pamphlets on masonry, mortar, adobe, aluminum and vinyl siding, glass, and many other topics. Write to your State Historic Preservation Officer for a complete list.

The U.S. Department of the Interior, Technical Preservation Services branch, has produced *Respectful Rehabilitation: Answers to Your Questions About Old Buildings*, rev. ed. (Washington, D.C.: Preservation Press, 1986). A more popular guide to renovation is *The Old-House Journal*, published since 1974 for owners of pre-1939 houses.

Several heavily illustrated children's books discuss house construction and building skills in basic terms. These include: Karin Kelly, *Carpentry* (Minneapolis: Lerner Publications Co., 1974); Arthur Shay, *What Happens When You Build a House* (Chicago: Reilly & Lee Books, 1970), and Harriet Langsam Sobol, *Pete's House* (New York: Macmillan Publishing Co., Inc., 1978).

The American Association for State and Local History sells several audio-visual presentations on topics related to building construction and household technology, including "Cleaning Masonry Buildings" (AV-414), "Hardware Restoration" (AV-411), "Historic House Paint Analysis" (AV-413), "Identification of Nineteenth-Century Domestic Lighting" (AV-415), "Identifying Energy Conservation Problems in Historic Houses" (AV-420), "Overall Planning for Historic House Restoration" (AV-403), "Preservation of Log Structures" (AV-412), "Reading a Building: Adobe" (AV-402), "Reading a Building: Colonial" (AV-401), "Solving Energy Conservation Problems in Historic Houses" (AV-421), "The Victorian House: Identification and Conservation" (AV-418), "Victorian House Colors: Exterior" (AV-404), and "Window Glass in Historic Houses" (AV-417).

·9·

Household Technology

MODERN UTILITIES, INTRODUCED IN THE COMMERCIAL and industrial cities of the nineteenth century, offer clues to the history of a house and its residents. The provision of pure water, electricity, gas, telephone, and telegraph services, and the disposal of both solid and liquid wastes for urban dwellers was a great triumph. These innovations profoundly influenced the home as well as the life style of its occupants. Understanding the evolution of utilities will help unravel the clues left behind in the form of piping, radiators, fireplaces, light fixtures, and bathroom or kitchen fixtures.

Suppliers' catalogues, such as those published by Sears, Roebuck and Co. or Montgomery Ward & Co., are invaluable to the house historian studying household technology. After Rural Free Delivery was instituted in 1893 and parcel post in 1913, people living in rural areas could order stoves, lighting fixtures, plumbing fixtures, or thousands of other products by mail.

Water Systems

Until the nineteenth century, piped water was unknown in most of North America. As a result, houses were located near convenient water supplies. Privies provided the means of disposing domestic waste. For widely scattered homesteads, this ancient system sufficed.

In crowded industrial cities, the privy system became grossly inadequate. Boston, New York, Philadelphia, Richmond, and other eastern cities had piped water in the first third of the nineteenth century. Limited progress was made in purifying and supplying water until, in 1854, London officials

127

Sears, Roebuck and Co.'s 1920 *Modern Plumbing* catalogue illustrated an indoor plumbing system for those who lived in areas not serviced by a central piped water supply. The materials could be purchased on credit, and "ANYONE, even if he'd never laid a pipe in his life, could do pretty nearly a perfect plumbing job if he followed the instructions."

proved beyond doubt that a cholera outbreak had spread from a single pump. This demonstration, coupled with Louis Pasteur's work on the germ theory of disease, led directly to a new technology to filter and treat drinking and waste water.

By the late nineteenth century, indoor plumbing was standard for most North American homes, except in rural communities and farmsteads. Gas-fired heaters provided running hot water, and plumbing "fittings" were mass produced. The extensive literature on styles of plumbing fixtures will help the house historian determine the approximate date of a building or remodeling effort from original fittings.

By 1900, most urban areas in North America enjoyed pure and plentiful water. This triumph of public health signaled a revolution in kitchen and bathroom design. Obsolete hand pumps, dry sinks, and privies were replaced by drains, flush toilets, and sinks and bathtubs featuring running hot and cold water. A network of sanitary sewers transported waterborne domestic and industrial wastes to the nearest river or stream.

Heating and Cooling Systems

House historians should look for clues to various methods used to heat and cool the house through its history. Is there a coal bin in the basement or a door on the outside through which coal could be shoveled into the house? Where were separate furnaces or other heating devices installed if a building was converted into apartments? Do fireplaces still exist or have they been covered over?

In colonial houses, the usual source of heat was the open fireplace. The design of the fireplace, strongly influenced by regional and ethnic traditions in vernacular housing types, is one of the most prominent features of many homes. Decorative gas-fired fireplaces indicated that the home owners could afford central heating. Home owners restoring historic homes with fireplaces should be careful to note whether they were originally intended to burn wood or coal, as coal-burning fireplaces were much smaller than those for wood.

During the nineteenth century, home heating improved with new, inexpensive, and compact iron heating stoves, which were used during cold weather in bedrooms and parlors and were removed, cleaned, and stored during hot weather. Iron stoves for cooking and heating were manufactured in vast numbers and in an amazing variety of styles and shapes. The iron stove tradition continues to this day with the efficient, air-tight wood-burning stoves that became popular after the energy crisis of the 1970s. In many older homes, central heating systems have replaced the old stoves. House historians may find telltale evidence of the stoves in the form of flue caps high on the wall or round openings in the chimney. Both hot air and radiator systems were perfected before the twentieth century and were widely used throughout the country except in the South.

Late nineteenth-century houses used large windows, transoms over doors, high ceilings, and careful alignment of windows and doors to maximize ventilation and natural lighting. By the mid-twentieth century, window size, door height, and ceiling height had decreased. In some large apartment buildings, windows were sealed shut, and residents were left with the climate-controlled environment produced by central heating and air conditioning.

Air conditioning was a logical extension of central heating. First, individual window units appeared, hardly pleasing embellishments to the exteriors of houses despite their useful purpose. Central air conditioning for buildings first appeared in theatres and cinemas and later spread to restaurants, shops, and office and apartment buildings. Only recently has it become a standard feature in house construction. Many older forced-air central furnaces have been converted to provide both heat and cooled, dehumidified air.

The increase in energy prices beginning in the mid-1970s and mounting public concern for saving natural resources promoted an awareness of the need for energy efficient buildings. Additional insulation was added to homes, both new and old. To install thicker, more efficient insulation, the traditional balloon frame has been modified to use two-by-six-inch studs spaced two feet apart rather than the traditional two-by-four-inch studs spaced sixteen inches apart. Solar collectors and other energy devices have changed the appearance of homes inside and out in very noticeable ways.

Lighting Systems

Candles, firelight, rush lamps, and various oil lamps illuminated colonial homes and served much of the United States's population into the nineteenth century. House historians may find candle molds and candlesticks or lamps in a home, but these left few permanent marks on the structure. In contrast, gas and, later, electricity, have left many clues for the diligent investigator.

Gas became the preferred means of lighting in American homes, factories, and commercial buildings in the 1830s. Early gas lighting fixtures were

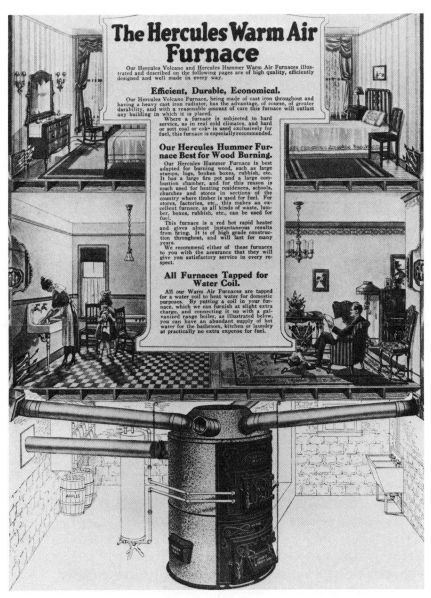

The advertisement reads:

The Hercules Warm Air Furnace

Our Hercules Volcano and Hercules Hummer Warm Air Furnaces illustrated and described on the following pages are of high quality, efficiently designed and well made in every way.

Efficient, Durable, Economical.

Our Hercules Volcano Furnace, being made of cast iron throughout and having a heavy cast iron radiator, has the advantage, of course, of greater durability, and with a reasonable amount of care this furnace will outlast any building in which it is placed.

Where a furnace is subjected to hard service, as in real cold climates, and hard or soft coal or coke is used exclusively for fuel, this furnace is especially recommended.

Our Hercules Hummer Furnace Best for Wood Burning.

Our Hercules Hummer Furnace is best adapted for burning wood, such as large stumps, logs, broken boxes, rubbish, etc. It has a large fire pot and a large combustion chamber, and for this reason is much used for heating residences, schools, churches and stores in sections of the country where timber is used for fuel. For stores, factories, etc., this makes an excellent furnace, as all kinds of waste, lumber, boxes, rubbish, etc., can be used for fuel.

This furnace is a red hot rapid heater and gives almost instantaneous results from firing. It is of high grade construction throughout, and will last for many years.

We recommend either of these furnaces to you with the assurance that they will give you satisfactory service in every respect.

All Furnaces Tapped for Water Coil.

All our Warm Air Furnaces are tapped for a water coil to heat water for domestic purposes. By putting a coil in your furnace, which we can furnish at slight extra charge, and connecting it up with a galvanized range boiler, as illustrated below, you can have an abundant supply of hot water for the bathroom, kitchen or laundry at practically no extra expense for fuel.

Sears, Roebuck and Co. advertised its Hercules Warm Air Furnace in a circa 1920 catalogue entitled *Modern Heating Systems*. In addition to showing how to install a furnace, the ad shows the furnishings that could be found in the house and illustrates the "proper" roles for those living there—mother and daughter washing the dishes while father and son relax in the living room.

simply open flames controlled by gas cocks. The fixtures provided low levels of illumination, emitting a rather pungent odor and considerable heat. The most notable of many improvements in globes and lamp mantles for gas fixtures was the incandescent mantle developed in Austria by Carl von Welsback in 1886; his idea is still used in modern camping lanterns. This brilliant light was an instant success and was so popular that it was a strong competitor to the electric light for several decades after its introduction.

The house historian can interpret the history of gas lighting through artifacts, in this case light fixtures. These practical devices were decorated to suit nearly every taste. The researcher may find gasoliers wired for electricity or, often, marks or capped pipes on the walls of a house where gas sconces had been located. By the end of the nineteenth century, natural gas began to replace town or manufactured gas. Natural gas was a superior fuel for heating and, with the development of cross-country pipe lines, was available in quantity at an economical price.

A knowledge of electrical distribution systems and fittings and of the introduction of electricity in a neighborhood can help the house historian date a building. And, because all of the components in electrical systems, including wire, were mass produced, the historican can find a wealth of information in catalogues and magazine advertisements pertaining to the systems.

Electricity remained a scientific curiosity with no practical application until the invention and perfection of the incandescent electric lamp and the electric motor. Until electrical power generation and distribution systems were built, neither the motor nor the lamp was capable of more than isolated application. America's first electric power plant was built in 1882 by the Edison Electric Company in New York, and the Columbian Exposition of 1893 in Chicago served as a powerful promoter of electricity to Americans.

By the end of World War I, electricity had replaced gas for lighting in towns and cities. Following the war, electricity powered a wide array of household appliances, which have become an accepted part of the American home. Electricity came to rural areas in America beginning in the 1930s. Then, farm families were able to enjoy the benefits of electricity through New Deal programs such as the Tennessee Valley Authority and Rural Electrification Administration.

Electric motors are found in many household appliances. The electric fan has been used in conjunction with forced-air heating, ventilating, and air conditioning. One may find ventilating fans in the form of square frames

fitted into the ceilings of rooms or replicas of early-twentieth-century sus-
pended ceiling fans. The elevator, driven by electric motors, made it feasible to erect buildings of more than four or five stories. While early hydraulic
elevators are occasionally found, the electric motor-driven elevator dominates
the field.

Homes are frequently subjected to modernization, which nearly always
involves upgrading existing utilities within the building or installing new
services. Such modifications are part of the evolution of any home, and the
house historian should take care to record them as part of the history of
the structure.

Suggested Readings

A number of sources are available to those interested in examining technology related
to plumbing, heating, air conditioning, electricity, lighting, and ventilation in the home.
The Committee on History and Heritage of the American Society of Civil Engineers published *Pure and Wholesome: A Collection of Papers on Water and Waste Treatment at the Turn
of the Century* (New York: American Society of Civil Engineers, 1982) to provide a background on the development of plumbing and sewage systems in the United States. One
case study of the impact of rural electrification on the home can be found in R. Douglas
Hurt, "REA: A New Deal for Farmers," *Timeline* 2 (January 1986): 32-47. Witold Rybczynski, in *Home: A Short History of an Idea* (New York: Viking, 1986), provides a broad perspective to the development of the idea of comfort in a home; his scope includes the
development of household technologies.

Reference works on home lighting include: Max Ferro and Melissa L. Cook, *Electric Wiring
and Lighting in Historic American Buildings: Guidelines for Restoration and Rehabilitation* (New
Bedford, Mass.: AFC / A Norteck Co., 1984); Larry Freeman, *New Light on Old Lamps*,
7th ed. (Watkins Glen, N.Y.: American Life Foundation—Century House Books, 1984);
Catherine M. Thuro, *Oil Lamps: The Kerosene Era in North America* (Lombard, Ill.: Wallace-
Homestead Book Co., 1976); and *A Glossary of Old Lamp and Lighting Devices*, American
Association for State and Local History Technical Leaflet 30, *History News* 20: 8 (August
1965).

A short guide to sinks can be found in J. Randall Cotton, "The Evolution of Sinks,"
The Old-House Journal 14 (August 1986): 270-278.

Local historical societies and museums as well as businesses may have catalogues of local,
regional, or national suppliers. Many companies market reproduction items for those renovating older homes. Catalogues from firms like Renovator's Supply Company are full of bathroom fixtures and lighting fixtures appropriate for older homes. Also, the staff of *The
Old-House Journal* annually publishes *The Old-House Buyer's Guide: A Complete Where-To
Guide for Old-House Lovers*, which tells renovators where to buy items and services for
pre-1939 homes.

Period catalogues are available in reprint form or on microfiche. The *Picture Book of*

Authentic Mid-Victorian Gas Lighting Fixtures is a reprint of Mitchell, Vance & Company's 1876 catalogue. *Victorian Lighting: The Dietz Catalogue of 1860* includes a history of the company and of Victorian lighting. Both are available through Victorian Accents (661 West Seventh Street, Plainfield, New Jersey 07060).

The Clearwater Publishing Company (1995 Broadway, New York, New York 10023) has produced "Trade Catalogues at Avery" and "Trade Catalogues at Winterthur," both microfiche collections covering products such as decorations and ornaments, linoleum, plumbing and heating fixtures, structural steel, prefabricated buildings, architectural ironwork, architectural building plans and materials, and wall coverings. The 2,300 catalogues now housed at the Avery Architectural and Fine Arts Library of Columbia University were published originally between the 1860s and 1950s, while the 1,885 entries from the Winterthur Museum date from 1750 to 1980.

University libraries, particularly those serving engineering or architectural schools, may have the *Architectural Catalog File*, published by Sweet's Catalog Service since 1906. A huge compendium of advertisements for everything architects may need to include in their buildings, the catalogue is an invaluable guide to products available.

·10·

Families at Home

COLONIAL HOMES AND CONDOMINIUMS THAT OPENED yesterday, and every home built in between, reflect the lives of their occupants. Family size and structure have shaped the history of housing. For example, the ages at which men and women marry determine the need for "singles" complexes. The rising average life expectancy has created the need for retirement homes. The number of children in a family and the differences in their ages affects how much room in the home is devoted to them.

The house historian can gain many insights on housing by studying family history. Historians of the American colonial period have examined vital statistics and community structures to explain family structure and status. Edmund S. Morgan, studying a Puritan society, found that a woman typically "gave up everything to her husband and devoted herself exclusively to managing his household." Morgan explored the ways in which theology defined all relationships. Single people, for example, were not allowed to live by themselves, and town officials monitored parents to see that they were properly fulfilling their duties to their children. Privacy was nonexistent in the small houses occupied by most families.

After the American Revolution, changes in women's lives began to be reflected in family structure and status. Mary Beth Norton found that women experienced new opportunities as ideas of equality began to be implemented. However, very few moved far beyond the traditional role of wife and mother.

Uses of the Home

For much of early American history, home and workplace were synony-
mous for most families. In rural America, farming operations usually have
centered around the home. On the frontier or in isolated areas, women and
men have worked together in the home and on the surrounding land. This
partnership has been basic to survival.

In colonial America, urban families tried to live relatively close to the
workplace because walking was the chief form of transportation for all but
the rich. Middle-class artisans often lived above, beside, or behind their shops.
As cities grew larger in size and population, living close to work was no
longer always so feasible or desirable. New England farm girls were among
the first new industrial workers. They moved to Lowell, Massachusetts, for
example, to work in the textile factories and to live in mill town boarding
houses. Elsewhere, families worked together in the mills. During the early
nineteenth century, urbanization and industrialization thus moved the United
States from a predominantly rural barter economy into a cash economy.
Increasingly, individuals worked outside the home to earn cash to buy goods
and services they could not produce for themselves or to increase their standard of living.

At the same time, the home achieved a place of high importance as an
anchor in a sea of turmoil. A "cult of true womanhood" defined women's
status in society by the virtues of piety, purity, domesticity, and submissive-
ness. This middle- and upper-class philosophy required that women remain
sheltered at home in a separate sphere while men ventured out into the
world of business. After 1820, urban growth produced a housing shortage,
and many people moved into apartment houses and hotels. Because servants were available to do the hard housework, upper-middle-class and upper-
class women had time to volunteer for a variety of reform movements, such
as saving prostitutes and promoting temperance. They transferred their domesticity from cleaning up the house to cleaning up the world.

The concept that women in "better families" must stay at home lasted
through the nineteenth century and has lingered for some urban women
until the late twentieth century. It was reflected in the endless round of
visiting that occupied urban upper-class women in the late nineteenth century. Victorian houses designed with large entry halls and formal parlors
accommodated these urban social rituals.

Other modifications to homes occurred in the nineteenth century as the life styles of their occupants changed. Rooms became very specialized, with separate living rooms, dining rooms, morning rooms, pantries, and laundries. Large entrance hallways housed extra furniture, and clothing hung on hall trees before closets were common. Some houses contained ballrooms, even though one sometimes had to climb two flights of narrow back stairs to reach them. Although clubs were available in large cities for men to entertain their male business friends, much entertaining took place in the home, sometimes in a hall area to save the living room carpet from wear. The living room may have served as the funeral parlor when necessary. Small upstairs bedrooms may well have been for maids, while apartments over the carriage house were for male or married servants.

Clearly, Victorian Americans sought privacy, in sharp contrast to colonial Americans. Because of the uncertainties of birth control and the prevailing attitude that women were uninterested in sex, some late-nineteenth-century houses had sliding doors between the bedrooms of husband and wife.

For poorer families, sweatshop tenements were common in large cities as the nineteenth century ended. Women could sew, make artificial flowers, and roll cigars at home while tending their children or putting them to work as helpers. Often immigrant women worked under the worst conditions because wages (paid by the number of pieces made) were low and housing conditions bad; yet they faced discrimination so strong that they could not find jobs in stores or offices. Also, some immigrant cultures frowned on women working outside the home.

Many women cared for lodgers or boarders in their own homes. During the mid-eighteenth century, travelers preferred to stay at lodging or boarding houses where they found more privacy than at public inns. By the early twentieth century, boarders and lodgers lived in large houses in middle-class neighborhoods or crowded apartments in cities. Boarders received meals with the host family, while lodgers just had sleeping rooms. Single male immigrants frequently lived with relatives or fellow countrymen because they wanted to adjust slowly to life in the foreign land, because there was not enough other housing available, or because they needed to save money to bring the rest of the family to the United States. Students or couples moving to new environments within the United States also boarded with families. Boarders and lodgers provided extra cash to the host family, but women carried most of the burden. As servants, housewives, or widows, they were responsible for the cleaning, cooking, and laundry that accompanied extra people in the home. The presence of lodgers and boarders may have caused some physical alteration to be done to the house, such as the installation of extra baths or the division of rooms to create additional bedrooms.

While many single people were boarders or lodgers, others made their homes in settlement houses, where young college-educated men and women lived and worked toward the improvement of urban conditions. The most famous of these settlement houses, Jane Addams' Hull House, is now a Chicago museum. The house typifies the conversion of a large single-family house to one shared by several unrelated people. Groups such as the Young Men's Christian Association, Young Women's Christian Association, the Roman Catholic Church, and Women's Christian Temperance Union built rooming houses to help new arrivals adjust to urban life. These buildings often became obsolete by the late twentieth century, as the need for this type of housing diminished.

House historians are likely to find evidence of women's traditional activities—basement fruit cellars stocked with canning jars, laundry tubs, built-in ironing boards, and kitchen stoves. In addition, the designs of kitchen spaces reflect women's activities. "Outshots," for example, began as lean-to kitchens on New England farmhouses. In the South, early kitchens were built as separate buildings to keep the heat and danger of fire away from the main house. Cooking, hauling water, house cleaning, sewing, weaving, child care, nursing, spinning, food preservation, and laundry occupied countless hours before modern labor-saving devices appeared in the twentieth century. However, some of the allegedly "labor saving" devices actually increased women's responsibilities because standards of cooking and cleanliness rose with the introduction of more complicated stoves and ceramic tile bathrooms.

Nineteenth- and early-twentieth-century feminists experimented with ideas on housing. Houses built without kitchens and apartment houses with common kitchens and play areas for children made strong statements about the status of women: women should not have to spend all their hours keeping house. Some of these houses still exist, although it is likely that kitchens have since been added.

During the 1920s, consumer appliances became common in urban areas, redirecting efforts of feminists and housing reformers from eliminating kitchens to planning kitchens with new stoves and refrigerators. Rural families were able to benefit from electric appliances after the Rural Electrification Administration began in the 1930s. There were few further attempts to design co-operative housing or central kitchens, and the use of the term "co-operative" changed as well—it came to mean an apartment house co-operatively owned by its residents.

The smaller houses built in the early twentieth century no longer had room for live-in help. At the same time, fewer families could afford or find help. Young white women, now better educated, pursued new retail and office jobs offering higher pay, fewer hours, and more independence. With fewer options, undereducated, minority, and immigrant women continue to work as domestic servants.

The post-World War II baby boom greatly increased America's population. As families grew, houses became more child-centered. Homes built during this time for the middle-class often had separate bedrooms for each child, family rooms and dens, and playground equipment in the yard. New homes for the wealthy were larger versions of middle-class homes in contrast to the late nineteenth century when the very wealthy often inhabited grand mansions with gold-plated hardware, while the middle-class occupied row-houses or detached small houses designed for simple living, instead of for lavish entertaining.

By the late twentieth century, rooms became less specialized than in the large houses of a century earlier. Living, dining, and kitchen areas flowed into each other, and their uses were defined less clearly. Separate entrance hallways disappeared because home entertaining was no longer formal. Two-car garages became common as it was assumed that families would need two cars to accommodate a suburban life style without available public transportation.

The home has continued to be a workplace for some people. The seamstresses, piano teachers, and laundresses working at home in the nineteenth-century city probably required minimal alterations to their homes to carry on their daily work. Late-twentieth-century home workers sell cosmetics, produce and sell crafts, teach music, tutor, care for children, stuff envelopes, operate small businesses such as beauty parlors, run insurance and accounting agencies, provide secretarial services, and operate contract history businesses from their homes. Some of these occupations may require alterations to the home, such as installing sinks for a beauty parlor or computer terminals for an insurance agency.

Status Symbol or Necessity?

Then, as now, people may buy a larger house than they need if they aspire to a higher social status or want to appear affluent. Swimming pools, professionally landscaped yards, expensive cars in the driveway, and signs posted by makers of security systems provide exterior signs of visible wealth. On the interior, wealth and high social status may be visible in works of art, rare books, and expensive furniture.

Status can also be measured in terms of appliances provided in the house. Microwave ovens or trash compactors began as "status" appliances in the 1970s but became widely available by the 1980s. These appliances, like earlier dishwashers and washing machines, were used first in the homes of the urban rich, then in middle-class and rural areas. One of the few appliances first introduced in rural areas was the satellite dish to improve television reception.

For many families, installing an indoor bathroom marked a major step forward in the family's social status, at least as it was reflected in housing. Housing companies were still advertising homes without indoor bathrooms in the 1920s, and people who grew up in rural areas in the 1950s and 1960s can remember the installation of an indoor bathroom or moving into a new house with these facilities as a major event in their lives.

Rural families also measure status by criteria other than the size or configuration of their home. Instead, the size of a barn and outbuildings and the quality of their maintenance, as well as the quality of farm machinery used, are important measures of success. Similarly, well-maintained fields reflect hard work, and successful farming techniques are admired more than home furnishings. Thus, house historians who garner more information about the barn and tractor than the house and appliances during an interview with a farm family may be gaining very important insights into the attitudes and status of the family.

The historical status of minorities and poor families cannot be measured easily today because much of the early housing for these groups has disappeared. Few slave cabins or tenant farmer cabins survive. However, many cities still retain a few blocks of the alley dwellings created in the nineteenth century for low-income urban residents. Photographs of slum housing and graphic descriptions from the papers of housing reformers, Progressive era publications such as *Arena* and *Survey,* and contemporary accounts such as Jacob Riis's *How the Other Half Lives* tell some of the story, but many of the buildings themselves have fallen to the bulldozer.

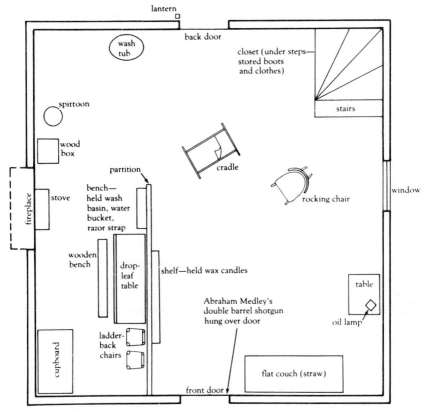

The Cusic-Medley house was probably built in the mid-nineteenth century. By interviewing members of the Medley family, George McDaniel was able to determine the furnishings and use of space when this black tenant family occupied the house in the 1920s.

The poor rarely had the option to build permanent housing as they wanted it. More often, they were tenants in someone else's property and had to adapt their life to the space they could afford. If they were slaves, housing was provided by their masters. Recent works on the black family give clues to family structure but do not discuss housing per se. In *Black Bostonians*, James and Lois Horton state that between 33 percent and 40 percent of that city's blacks between 1850 and 1860 took in boarders, many of whom were members of the extended family. This practice was both an economic and social necessity because most of Boston's hotels and boarding houses were for "whites only."

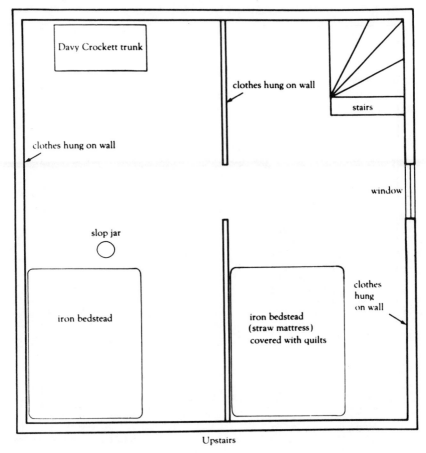

Upstairs

The upstairs of the Cusic-Medley house in the 1920s shows how space was partitioned to provide privacy. The parents slept in the room on the left while the four children shared the room on the right.

Public housing built after 1930 reflects particular attitudes toward family life. The poor in slums have had little privacy because of overcrowded conditions. In trying to improve housing for the poor, reformers sometimes moved people used to a "street culture" into high-rise apartment blocks.

New types of housing in the late twentieth century included high-rise apartments for senior citizens and childless couples. Many senior citizen housing projects received federal funding, allowing even small cities to have high- or mid-rise apartment buildings for them. At the same time, "swinging singles" apartment complexes with extensive recreational facilities catered to young people living alone or with roommates of their own age. The increasing options in housing make it possible for individuals to find shelter that reflects their family structure and status.

Suggested Readings

Colonial family references come from Edmund S. Morgan, *The Puritan Family: Religion and Domestic Relations in Seventeenth-Century New England*, 1944, rev. ed. (New York: Harper & Row, 1966); pp. 42, 132-160. For information on the post-Revolutionary War family, see Mary Beth Norton, *Liberty's Daughters: The Revolutionary Experience of American Women, 1750-1800* (Boston: Little, Brown and Co., 1980), pp. 34-35. For a discussion of "the cult," see Barbara Welter, "The Cult of True Womanhood: 1800-1860," in Barbara Welter, *Dimity Convictions: The American Woman in the Nineteenth Century* (Athens: Ohio University Press, 1976), pp. 21-41. For background on feminism and urbanism, see Barbara Berg, *The Remembered Gate: Origins of American Feminism, The Woman & The City, 1800-1860* (Oxford: Oxford University Press, 1978). For information on co-operative housing experiments, see Dolores Hayden, *Grand Domestic Revolution: A History of Feminist Designs for American Homes, Neighborhoods, and Cities* (Cambridge, Mass.: The MIT Press, 1981). For information on housing of blacks, see George W. McDaniel, *Hearth and Home: Preserving a People's Culture* (Philadelphia: Temple University Press, 1982) and James and Lois E. Horton, *Black Bostonians: Family Life and Community Struggle in the Antebellum North* (New York: Holmes & Meier, Inc. 1979).

Other general histories of the family and histories of women that deal with family status include Carl Degler, *At Odds: Women and the Family in America from the Revolution to the Present* (New York: Oxford University Press, 1980); Michael Gordon, *The American Family in Social-Historical Perspective*, 3rd ed. (New York: St. Martin's Press, 1973); Colleen McDannell, *The Christian Home in Victorian America, 1840-1900* (Bloomington, Ind.: Indiana University Press, 1986); Theodore K. Robb and Robert I. Rotberg, *The Family in History: Interdisciplinary Essays* (New York: Harper & Row, 1971); Mary P. Ryan, *Womanhood in America from Colonial Times to the Present*, 3rd ed. (New York: Franklin Watts, 1983); and Donald M. Scott and Bernard Wishy, eds., *America's Families: A Documentary History* (New York: Harper & Row, 1982). Relevant journals include the *Journal of Family History* and the *Journal of Social History*.

Colonial women are discussed in Elisabeth Anthony Dexter, *Colonial Women of Affairs: Women in Business and the Professions in America Before 1776*, 2nd ed. (Boston: Houghton Mifflin Co., 1931); Elisabeth Anthony Dexter, *Career Women of America, 1776-1840*, 1950 (Clifton: Augustus M. Kelley, 1972); Julia Cherry Spruill, *Women's Life & Work in the Southern Colonies*, 1938 (New York: W. W. Norton & Co., 1972); and Laurel Thatcher Ulrich, *Good Wives: Image and Reality in the Lives of Women in Northern New England, 1650-1750*, 2nd ed. (New York: Oxford University Press, 1982).

Sources on women's work, both inside and outside the home, include Catharine Beecher, *A Treatise on Domestic Economy*, 1841 (New York: Shocken Books, 1977); Ruth Schwartz Cowan, *More Work for Mother: The Ironies of Household Technology from the Open Hearth* to the Microwave (New York: Basic Books, 1983); Faye E. Dudden, *Serving Women: House-hold Service in Nineteenth-Century America* (Middletown, Conn.: Wesleyan University Press, 1983); Alice Kessler-Harris, *Women Have Always Worked: A Historical Overview* (Old Westbury, N.Y.: Feminist Press, 1981); Annegret S. Ogden, *The Great American Housewife: From Helpmate to Wage Earner, 1776-1986* (Westport, Conn.: Greenwood Press, 1986); John Stilgoe, *Common Landscape of America, 1580 to 1845* (New Haven: Yale University Press, 1982); Susan Strasser, *Never Done: A History of American Housework* (New York: Pantheon Books, 1982); and Barbara Mayer Wertheimer, *We Were There: The Story of Working Women in America* (New York: Pantheon Books, 1977).

Rural women are discussed in Catherine Clinton, *The Plantation Mistress: Women's World in the Old South* (New York: Pantheon, 1982); Julie Roy Jeffrey, *Frontier Women: The Trans-Mississippi West, 1840-1880* (New York: Hill and Wang, 1979); Joan M. Jensen, *With These Hands: Women Working on the Land* (Old Westbury, N.Y.: Feminist Press, 1981); and Cecelia Hendricks Wahl, ed., *Letters from Honeyhill: A Woman's View of Homesteading, 1914-1931* (Boulder, Colo.: Pruett Publishing Co., 1986).

General information on farming practices may be available in agricultural journals or publications such as the "Foxfire" series. Robert W. Miller's *Pictorial Guide to Early American Tools and Implements* (Des Moines: Wallace Homestead Book Co., 1980) is one of many books available on tools and farm implements. *Farmer's and Housekeeper's Cyclopedia / 1888* provides information on nineteenth-century farming techniques and household patterns; it is available as a reprint from ASAE, Department 250, 2950 Niles Road, St. Joseph, Michigan 49085-9659.

Helpful works on the black family include Ira Berlin, *Slaves Without Masters: The Free Negro in the Antebellum South* (New York: Pantheon Books, 1974); John W. Blassingame, *The Slave Community: Plantation Life in the Ante-Bellum South* (New York: Oxford University Press, 1972); Eugene D. Genovese, *Roll, Jordan, Roll: The World the Slaves Made* (New York: Pantheon Books, 1974); Paula Giddings, *When and Where I Enter: The Impact of Black Women on Race and Sex in America* (Toronto: Bantam Books, 1984); and Robert Staples, ed., *The Black Family: Essays and Studies* (Belmont, Calif.: Wadsworth Publishing Co., 1970). Information on the use of demographic data to re-create households is available in "Appendix A" and "Appendix B: Black, Jewish, and Italian Households in New York City, 1905," in Herbert G. Gutman's *The Black Family in Slavery and Freedom, 1750-1925* (New York: Pantheon Books, 1976), pp. 477-530. Gutman's pioneering work discusses household composition but not housing.

Sources on poor families and immigrant families include Charlotte Baum, Paula Hyman, and Sonya Michel, *The Jewish Woman in America* (New York: New American Library, 1975, 1976); James Borchert, *Alley Life in Washington: Family, Community, Religion, and Folklife in the City, 1800-1970* (Urbana: University of Illinois Press, 1980); Margaret Byington, *Homestead: The Households of a Mill Town, 1910* (Pittsburgh: University of Pittsburgh, 1974); Oscar Handlin, *The Uprooted* (New York: Grosset and Dunlap, 1957); Irving Howe, *World of Our Fathers* (New York: Harcourt Brace Jovanovich, 1976); Jacob Riis, *How the Other Half Lives, 1890* (New York: Hill and Wang, 1957); Virginia Yans-McLaughlin, *Family and Community: Italian Immigrants in Buffalo, 1880-1930* (Ithaca: Cornell University Press, 1977); and numerous articles in journals such as *Survey* for the early twentieth century.

M. Christine Anderson's "Home and Community for a Generation of Women: A Case Study of the Cincinnati Y.W.C.A. Residence, 1920-1940," in *Queen City Heritage* 43 (Winter 1985): 34-41, details the occupations of women living at the YWCA and the home-like atmosphere they found there.

Diaries, letters, or women's magazines may discuss women's domestic attitudes and activities. From the early nineteenth century onward, cookbooks and child rearing manuals are rich sources of insight. Blue Books and Social Registers often indicated "at home" days, while etiquette guides explain the elaborate rituals associated with calling cards and visiting. These sources are useful for understanding how people perceived their homes.

For perhaps the "ultimate" history of a house and its inhabitants, see William Seale, *The President's House: A History*, 2 vols. (Washington, D.C.: White House Historical Association with the cooperation of the National Geographic Society and Henry N. Abrams, Inc., 1986).

For a contemporary view of housing, family structure, and status, magazines such as *Better Homes and Gardens* will give an idea of the life one should be living in a particular type of house. Popular news magazines such as *Time* and *Newsweek* or feature magazines such as *Ms.* and *Working Woman* include articles on patterns in American society, including the changing roles of men and women in the home.

·11·

Putting Together a House History

ASSEMBLING A HOUSE HISTORY IS LIKE PUTTING together pieces of a puzzle. What do the clues tell us? What don't they reveal? Where do they mesh together perfectly? Where do they conflict? Having discussed sources of information, research techniques, and questions to be considered, we believe it best to conclude, not with more advice, but with an illustration of the possibilities awaiting a house historian. Therefore, we present below a condensed version of a house history prepared by Ruth Ann Overbeck. Included in it are references to the sources used to prepare this history and to earlier chapters in this book that contain general discussions of the concepts applied in this case study.

517 East Capitol Street, S.E., Washington, D.C.
Square 841, Lot 807

When Washington, D.C. was created in 1790, George Washington requested landowners within the proposed city limits to embark on an adventure filled with financial peril. By yielding to the government's plans, most of the original land owners and several generations of subsequent speculators endured heartbreak and financial loss.

The plan called for the release of the owners' rural properties. In exchange, the federal government would give them the following: a plat of their land showing the layout of streets, city squares (blocks) divided into lots and alleys, and grounds to be reserved for public buildings and parks; payment for half of the lots created in the city squares; and assignment back to the owners of the other half by the federal government. The owners could then sell or retain the lots as they and the market dictated.

Significant short-term adversity lay ahead for the land owners. The government marketed the lots it kept in direct competition with the private owners; it did not compensate them for the land used for streets, alleys, public buildings, or grounds; nor did it permit them to engage in large-scale agricultural endeavors within the city limits. To oversee the infant capital city and the surrounding federal district, the federal government appointed a group known informally as the D.C. Commissioners. [Local histories summarize the city's creation. Records of the D.C. Commissioners contain primary sources such as letters and minutes of meetings. See chapter 4 for information on locating and using such sources.]

Through this process, square 841 was platted. William Prout owned the land from which it was carved. Prout was not typical of the city's first proprietors—elite families who had owned the land for generations. Born about 1755, Prout became a respected Baltimore merchant. He moved to the District of Columbia shortly after 1790 and established a general merchandise store in Georgetown. By 1795, he advertised the business for sale and relocated on Capitol Hill near his wife's ancestral home. Prout's acquisition of Capitol Hill land and his marriage to Sarah Slater appear to be strongly linked. [Information on Prout was derived from contemporary newspapers and censuses; again, see chapter 4. Prout family ages are derived from tombstones.]

In September 1795, Prout signed the Division Agreement that transferred square 841 to the federal government. Over the next few years, the property changed hands several times. First, New England speculator James Greenleaf acquired the rights to hundreds of city lots, including all those in square 841. He then mortgaged the lots to a European consortium dominated by Dutch businessmen and bankers. Because the consortium could not raise all the money necessary, it released some lots, among them square 841, almost immediately. [Deeds and records of the D.C. Commissioners contain land transaction information. Local histories have details of the speculation activities. These sources are discussed in chapter 4.]

The square's last eighteenth-century owner was a Philadelphia-based real estate speculation combine of Robert Morris and John Nicholson. The two owners declared bankruptcy; law suits followed; and square 841 was one of the properties listed in an equity case settled in 1810. [See the case study on Friendship House in chapter 5; Duncanson's bankruptcy is tied to these transactions.] In the settlement, square 841 and other land totaling 1.5 million square feet were awarded to five Philadelphians, with Edward Shippen Burd acting as trustee for the group. At that time, no building stood on square 841. Then, and for several decades, the square's location five blocks east of the U.S. Capitol was too far removed from the nucleus of population to interest most speculators or developers. The Philadelphians, however, were used to holding large quantities of land in hopes of a profit. Burd, for instance, was related to the Shippen brothers, some of the first Americans to encourage suburban development on a significant scale. Thus, square 841 remained unimproved in the hands of its absentee owners. [Court cases, deeds, and tax records contain information on the land transfers and the lack of improvements. Carl Bridenbaugh noted the Shippens's activities in *Cities in the Wilderness*. Refer to chapter 6 for more information about land use and speculation.]

In 1839, Charles H. Miller, a Washington butcher, bought three-quarters of square 841 plus thirteen other Capitol Hill lots, all unimproved and all within five blocks of the Capitol. As befitted his occupation, one then considered a "nuisance," he lived somewhat removed from his nearest neighbors. (A restrictive covenant written in the 1850s for a suburb of Washington forbade "nuisance" industries such as piggeries and slaughterhouses. The covenant made lawful what was already customary, locating such sites away from population centers.) Miller died sometime before 1860, but his estate remained unsettled for a decade. [Deeds and tax records yield real estate information; censuses and city directories include information on the family. See chapter 4 for a discussion of these sources.]

After the Civil War, Washington changed dramatically. Official Washington had to reunite the divided nation and cope with an enormous influx of people: veterans, war widows, and orphans seeking jobs; northern war profiteers trying to keep alive government contracts acquired during the war; and emancipated slaves and European immigrants searching for new homes. Housing was scarce, and a building boom ensued. New residential construction moved outward from the old population centers. [Local histories cover the broad scope of development. Insurance maps provide a way to measure and compare extant housing density, and tax records document the immediate neighborhood. See chapters 2 and 4 for background on these sources and techniques.]

The trustees of Miller's estate subdivided several lots in square 841. The new parcel they designated as lot 19 was larger than the city's average subdivided lot. It measured 21 feet wide by 138 feet deep, faced north, and was one lot in from the corner of East Capitol Street and Sixth Street, South East. [Deeds and plats provide these details.]

Hugh McCaffrey entered the history of square 841 in 1870 when he purchased two of its subdivided vacant lots. He paid a total of $2,148.77 for lot 19 and the corner lot, lot 20. This substantial sum reflects the speculative aura then prevalent in Washington as well as the potential of the oversized lots to be subdivided further.

Documentation on McCaffrey is contradictory. Three different birth dates indicate that he was born in Maryland, probably in 1822. The son of Irish-born parents, he moved to Washington and worked as a machinist. When the 1850 census was taken, both he and a machinist from Germany were boarding in the Nicholas Sanderson household. Nearly all the household's men, including McCaffrey, worked at the nearby Navy Yard. Sometime before 1858, McCaffrey married Irish-born Kate and fathered at least four children before 1870. The McCaffreys profited in the expansive economy in Washington. By the war's end, they owned a grocery-liquor store advertised in city directories as late as 1871. [City directories, 1860-1875, and census records, 1850-1880.]

During 1872 and 1873, McCaffrey had a matched pair of Victorian flat front rowhouses built on lots 19 and 20. How involved he was with their actual construction is unclear. Once the East Capitol Street houses were complete, however, he gave his occupation as "house contractor" and no longer listed his store in city directories. (McCaffrey's early use of the title "house contractor" is one of this house history's most significant "finds." Washington's building tradesmen lagged decades behind those in other eastern cities in adopting the term.) When new, the tax assessor valued the three-story-plus-basement house at 517 East Capitol Street at $4,000 and its lot at $1,305. These sums represented a solidly upper-middle range of Capitol Hill's middle-class housing for the era, and the building confirms that status. [Tax records establish construction date and valuation as well as comparative data.]

McCaffrey's houses were built in the version of bracketed Italianate style that had begun to sweep Washington by 1870. The bricks on the flatfront facades were laid in running bond, reminiscent of the older Federal style. Ornamental brackets at the roofline cornices and door hoods, decorative sawn work applied to the entablatures, the front door's pair of two-panel vaults, and the tall windows with two-lite sashes belong to Washington's bracketed Italianate period. Most of the original fabric of 517 East Capitol's

1. Entablature
2. Rowhouse party wall obscured by continuous brick facade
3. Italiante bracket with drip pendant
4. Sawn wood applique
5. Two-lite-over-two-lite double hung sashes
6. Door hood of cornice supported by ornamental brackets
7. Pair of two panel vaults
8. Marble stoop

517 East Capitol Street, S.E., Washington, D.C. Built 1872-1873.

facade remains intact, in excellent condition. Its red pressed bricks were not intended to be painted, but numerous trim colors would have been appropriate. [See chapter 2 for architectural dictionaries, chapter 3 for information on examining a home's exterior, and chapter 5 for the use of photographs as documents.]

Slight differences distinguish this floor plan from those of Washington's pre-Civil War rowhouses, notably the inclusion of a foyer. Once inside the foyer's inner doors, the first floor layout contained a side stairhall running alongside the double parlor and terminating at the dining room door. The kitchen occupied the rear of the first story. On the second floor, the master bedroom and adjacent clothes room spanned the front of the house. Four smaller rooms opened onto the long side hall, which led to the rear second floor door. By contrast, the third story was only two rooms deep. [Historic American Buildings Survey's collection of Washington residential floor plans and years of on-site research provide a data base for comparisons. See chapter 10 for general comments on Victorian use of space.]

The interior decor was in the latest middle-class Victorian fashion. Twelve-foot high ceilings gave the first floor hall and rooms a sense of expansiveness, and the ceilings themselves contained elaborate plaster ceiling medallions from which gas-lit chandeliers were hung. Original light fixtures were removed years ago, but the large medallions remain gloriously intact. A pair of plaster doves, an unusual design element in Washington's extant Victorian houses, grace the hall's diamond shaped medallion. The circular medallions in the parlor and dining room are the more usual floral motifs. Deeply curved crown moldings contained an inch-wide band of waterlaid gilding. Pine paneling facing the side of the staircase was first calcimined, then stained and faux grained to simulate oak and a pair of faux marbled slate mantels surrounded the coal grates in the parlor fireplaces. Only the dining room's original wallpaper pattern is known. Predominantly white on a deep red background, its bold rococo pattern repeated at approximately two-foot intervals. [See chapter 3 for techniques on examining the interior of a home.]

Several mysteries remain about the original design of the house. Its interior rear staircase between the first and second floors apparently opened into the dining room rather than into the kitchen as most of Washington's known rear stairs did. McCaffrey may have presumed the house would have boarders who would want direct access to the dining room from their second floor bedrooms.

Many Washington houses of the era were built with indoor bathrooms.

At 517 East Capitol, an exterior wooden staircase led from the second story rear to the ground. Fitted underneath the staircase at grade level was a small closet-like room, entered by a door with a quarter moon carved in it. Unlike privies, the enclosure had no built-in bench. Was this adjunct built to hold a chair fitted with a chamber pot? If so, did it supplement the indoor toilet at the rear of the second floor or was the house built without an interior bathroom? [By 1865, real estate ads in Washington newspapers cited indoor bathrooms in some new construction. See chapter 4 for information on using newspapers in research and chapter 9 for information on plumbing systems.]

The concrete basement floor raises another question. Cement or concrete was relatively new to Washington's building industry in 1872 and certainly was not used routinely in middle-class residences. Modern Portland cement was not available in the city before 1890. Therefore, if the floor is original, it would have been cast with natural cement. [Chemical analysis of a core sample from the floor would determine content and date the concrete. See chapters 3 and 8 for information on interior features and construction techniques.]

Once the pair of houses was completed, McCaffrey moved his family into the corner building and rented out 517 East Capitol. The earliest tenants were members of the Nicholas Sanderson family with whom McCaffrey himself had lived almost thirty years before. Catharine Sanderson, Nicholas's widow, and all her children were at least third-generation native Washingtonians. Six of the at least ten Sanderson siblings moved to East Capitol Street with their mother. Mrs. Sanderson died shortly thereafter, and John W., the only known son, moved elsewhere on Capitol Hill. [City directories and censuses have family and mobility data.]

The house continued to be full of Sandersons, however. Nine people lived there when the 1880 census was taken. The census states that Hannah Sanderson was single and twenty-five years old. Working as a clerk in the U.S. Treasury Department, Hannah faced a four-mile roundtrip commute. She likely made the trip via the streetcars, which connected Capitol Hill to the White House, the Treasury, and other executive offices. [Local histories and streetcar route maps are described in chapters 4 and 5.]

Hannah was listed as head of the household despite the fact that she was not the oldest person in residence. Agnes, at twenty-seven, was "keeping house" for the brood, a position that evidently demoted her status below that of wage earner. The rest of the adult females in the house were Agnes and Hannah's sisters: Mary, twenty-three and a teacher; Rosa and Evelyn, twenty-one and nineteen respectively and with no occupations given; and Ellen, thirty-two, the only wife and mother among the siblings. George Castell, Ellen's husband, was a mechanical engineer who had been unemployed for half of 1879. We have no clue to the reason the Sanderson women retained such control that Castell was not listed as head of their household. More typically he or his wife, rather than Hannah, would have assumed that position following Catharine's death. Also, no information exists about how the Castells and their year-old daughter Nannie found some privacy or where Katie Hogan, the twelve-year-old niece and schoolgirl who completed the household, fit in. [1880 census. See chapter 10 for further information on family structure.]

In 1886 John H. Rogers acquired the residence and front eighty-four feet of lot 19. McCaffrey had subdivided lots 19 and 20 by lopping off the rear of each lot. In 1887 he apparently used proceeds from his sale to Rogers to build two more rowhouses on the new rear lots. [Land division and transfers appear in deeds and plat books, and building permits, implemented in Washington in 1877-1878, give dates for the new houses.]

Rogers and his wife Roseanne became 517's first owner-occupants. They moved from New York to Washington shortly after 1880. Like the Sandersons, their income came from government employment. Rogers, a political appointee, held several different positions with the House of Representatives before becoming one of their printing clerks. He must have been sure of his relationship with Congress; in 1882 *The Evening Star*, a local newspaper, noted that most government clerks hesitated to buy housing in Washington. Rather, they preferred to board or rent because of the uncertainty of the tenure of their appointments. [See chapter 4 for information about newspaper research.]

Rogers's earning power remained stable for almost a decade after he purchased 517 East Captiol. His annual salary ranged from $2,500 to $2,912, depending on whether or not Congress voted bonuses to its employees. In 1895 a former member of Congress replaced Rogers's boss as chief clerk of the House of Representatives, and Rogers no longer had a job. His only known job that year was during March when he tallied votes for Congress. [Payroll information from House of Representatives monthly reports provided information of Rogers's employment history. See chapter 4.]

When he died at the turn of the century, Rogers's will left the family home to his wife, daughter Annie, and a sister-in-law, who had predeceased him. His heirs had to cope with two deeds of trust that Rogers negotiated in 1895.

Although the mortgages were supposed to have been paid off in 1897, Roseanne Rogers did not receive their release papers until she sold the house in 1905. She evidently applied some of the sale proceeds to the mortgages, then moved to a nearby rental property. [See deeds, city directories, and probate records as described in chapter 4.]

In November 1905, John Warner, a widower, purchased 517 East Capitol. Because of the commoness of his name and lack of other identification, such as a wife's name, Warner cannot be traced biographically. Apparently neither he nor his heir(s) ever occupied the premises, but their forty years of ownership are the longest yet recorded for the property. During most of that time, they had the same tenants. [Land transfer information and John Warner's widower status appear in deeds.]

About 1910, Henry F. Belt and his wife Roberta, or "Bertie" as she was nicknamed, moved into Warner's house. A carpenter, Belt exemplifies Capitol Hill's history of being home to a sizeable segment of Washington's building trades population. Belt died about 1918, but his widow lived on in the big house until at least 1948. [The National Register nomination for the Captiol Hill Historic District contains an occupational summary for the area. City directories contain limited data.]

City directories carry no evidence that Bertie Belt had anyone living with her, but do state that many of her neighbors ran boarding houses or "tourist homes." Fragmentary information, however, proves conclusively that both family and paying "guests" resided with her. Her sister, Mrs. Lucy Minor, was a long-time member of the household. None of the numerous postcards and letters that turned up during a 1983-1984 rehabilitation of the building were addressed to Lucy, but "Cousin Bertie's" correspondents invariably asked her to pass on their regards to her sister. Some of the letters referred to the hard work the two women had to do and how tired they must be at day's end. One pointed to a long period of rooming house operation by noting that Bertie's decision to switch to taking in "tourists" instead of "regulars" should ease the burden.

The women were not without help. Laundry slips confirm that at least two bundles a week were sent out. When an unidentified Cecelia Graves was too pressed with her own duties to work at Mrs. Belt's, she sent a note recommending its bearer, an unnamed young girl who wanted work, as her temporary replacement.

In all probability, Mrs. Belt provided "board" as well as rooms. Receipts indicate that a local dairy regularly delivered substantial quantities of butter, milk, and eggs and that Mrs. Belt purchased fresh produce and poultry directly from rural suppliers, who also delivered. A note sent one Friday alerted Mrs. Belt that there were only two more young chickens and, at 5 1/4 and 4 1/2 pounds, they were not quite as heavy as those being delivered that day. The poultry raiser, "Grace," then added that she did not think the chickens would gain much during the ensuing week. In closing, Grace requested Mrs. Belt to drop her a card stating whether or not to send the chickens the next Friday. [Chapter 10 discusses background sources for the home as a workplace.]

Invitations, birth announcements, and notices about Presbyterian church events provide glimpses of life at 517 East Capitol Street. Most of the correspondence focused on the weather, travels, social gatherings, and family heartaches and illnesses. Letters from a cousin in Houston were the exception. Beginning in the summer of 1939, more than two years before the United States officially entered World War II, the cousin expressed grave concern about the upcoming war. A final letter, postmarked June 12, 1947, contained the cousin's sympathetic response to Bertie's announcement that she had to leave the house, which had been her home for so long.

Mrs. Belt's departure coincided with a change of ownership for 517 East Capitol. At the war's end in 1945, Richard A. Warner, John Warner's heir, sold the East Capitol Street property to Rose J. Waggaman. Both Warner and Waggaman lived across the city from Capitol Hill. Waggaman, however, was a secretary who worked next door to 517 East Capitol Street—at the real estate firm of Joseph Herbert and Sons. [Deeds and city directories provide cursory information about this period.]

Mrs. Belt continued to live at 517 East Capitol until the property changed hands again in March 1947. Its new owners were the Joseph Herberts, owners of the next door real estate firm. Mrs. Belt moved sometime before September 1948. That was when the first building permits for the house were issued. One was for plumbing, the other for the construction of two new "non-bearing partitions." The permits gave no locations for the partitions, but physical evidence abounds to show a bathroom was installed in a corner of the dining room. [See chapter 4 for information on building permits.]

These efforts to facilitate a multifamily use were made almost concurrently with the first documentable interest in the neighborhood as a historic area. History was repeating itself. Those squares closest to the Capitol drew immediate attention—this time from preservationists and speculators. A location five blocks from the Capitol seemed far away, but change was coming. [Contemporary newspapers and reminiscences of realtors document this period of transition. General information about these types of sources may be found in chapters 4 and 5.]

In 1950 Herman F. and Louise T. Karasek purchased 517 East Capitol Street. For the second time in its history, the house was owner occupied, and for the first time in about fifty years, children were part of the household. The adult Karaseks came to Washington to work for the federal government, in this instance the Department of Commerce. He was from South Dakota; she, from Oklahoma. They each received college degrees before leaving their home states. The couple moved to Capitol Hill during World War II and had lived nearby before they purchased 517 East Capitol Street.

The decade of the fifties was a busy one for the Karaseks. First, Herman resigned from the Department of Commerce to work in Congressman Francis Case's successful campaign for a Senate seat. When the election ended, Herman decided he needed the time to work on the rental properties he and Louise were amassing and to continue his real estate sales activities. From 1950 to 1956, the Karaseks owned and operated a nearby convenience or "Mom and Pop" store. In a familiar pattern for post-World War II Capitol Hill residents, the Karaseks accumulated a significant amount of real estate and at one time owned nineteen properties in Washington and nearby Maryland and Virginia.

Louise Karasek's career typifies that of many World War II-era professional women. Although she arrived in Washington with both B.S. and M.A. degrees in foreign languages, her occupation invariably appears as secretary. When her three daughters were born, between 1942 and 1945, Louise Karasek resigned from the Department of Commerce to raise them. She participated in civic organizations, PTAs, and especially the nearby Metropolitan Baptist Church. While her daughters were young, Louise worked with her husband in their home-based insurance agency, on some aspects of their real estate investments, and ultimately eased back into the outside work world, first as a substitute teacher, then as a full-time teacher. In 1960, with her daughters almost grown, Louise Karasek returned to work at the Department of Commerce as a secretary and staff aide. Herman Karasek continued as a part-time real estate agent. One of Washington's last city directories lists both Karaseks as retired, but still living at 517 East Capitol Street, S.E., in 1970. By 1983 they decided to move to Florida. When the property passed from the Karaseks, it marked the end of the second longest ownership. [Letters and interviews of Louise Karasek, and city directories document the Karaseks's occupancy.]

A late-twentieth-century life style ensued for the occupants of 517 East Capitol Street. Gone were the last of its roomers. Its new owners, Zorita and Richard Simunek, both have multifaceted careers. Like most of the previous owners, the Simuneks came to Washington to begin their careers with the federal government, he as an agricultural economist, she as a graphic designer. Their avocation of real estate investment and rehabilitation subsequently turned into a full time profession for Zorita, and in 1985 Richard became a consulting economist.

The Simuneks's approach to the house was to get to know it. They first determined that the bathroom which had been installed in part of the dining room in 1948 was expendable. It was removed, and the kitchen was gutted. A partition wall dividing the double parlor was removed. At that point, clue after clue emerged.

The parlor had been partitioned so long ago that the plaster crown moldings had not been painted before the partition was installed. With the wall removed, the waterlaid gilding in the crown molding became apparent. Evidence of each tread of the rear staircase was visible on the brick kitchen wall, and the dining room door leading to it still hung on its hinges. A circa 1900 mantel had been installed against the dining room wall. After it was removed, the Simuneks discovered a wealth of paperwork from Mrs. Belt's residency. The mantel evidently had been her favorite place to store important papers. Laundry and dairy receipts as well as other bits of the house's social history emerged. The dining room wallpaper also came to light when the plaster ceiling had to be replaced. The imprint of the wallpaper pattern showed clearly against the ceiling plaster when the last layer of paper was removed. The pattern was identical to fragments found on the wall.

Slowly, but surely, the history of the house surfaces. It is a history that illuminates the time, place, and people the house has served.

Comparative data on building contractors came from Melissa McLoud, "Craftsmen and Entrepreneurs: Builders in Late Nineteenth Century Washington" (Ph.D. dissertation, George Washington University, 1987).

Index

Correspondence: 517 E. Capitol documented in, 148, 155, 156, 158; of Albert Gallatin, 26, 28-29

Country clubs, 10, 44

Court cases: divorce, 53; 517 E. Capitol documented by, 149; insanity, 48, 53, 55; law suits, 53, 55, 148; probate, 45, 48, 53, 55, 155; mentioned, 48. *See also* Public records

Courtyard, 106

Covenants, restrictive, 51

"Cult of true womanhood," 136

Cultural hearths: Chesapeake Bay, 101-102; Colorado Plateau, 106; Delaware Valley, 102-103; definition of, 97; Hudson River Valley, 103-104; Mexican settlement, 106; Mississippi Delta, 105; Russian settlement, 106; St. Lawrence Valley, 104-105; Southern New England, 100-102; Southern Tidewater, 104; Utah Oasis, 106. *See also* House types

Dallas, Texas, 12

Date of construction, determining: for Hilly Grove farm, 64; for Capitol Hill houses, 72, 154; from construction, 109, 112, 115, 118, 120, 123; from utilities, 129, 132

Davis, Alexander Jackson, 81

Daytona Beach, Florida, 10

Deeds: court cases noted in, 53, 55; deeds of foreclosure, 48; deeds of trust, 154, 155; documenting names in, 45; dower statement in, 48; encumbrances in, 51; for 517 E. Capitol, 148, 149, 150, 154, 155, 156; guides to research in, 47; indexes to, 47; information found in, 46; quit claim, 51. *See also* Public records

Delaware Valley hearth, 102-103. *See also* Cultural hearths, House types

Demography, 10

Demonstration Cities and Metropolitan Development Act, 91

Description by plat. *See* Subdivision plat

Developers, 43, 88. *See also* Speculators

Diaries, 44

Dixon, Jeanne, 65

Divorce case files, 53. *See also* Court cases, Public records

Doctoral dissertations, 42, 89

Doors: bedroom, 137; changes in, 24, 25, 32-33, 98; at 517 E. Capitol, 150; as features of house types, 98, 105; in log buildings, 110; for ventilation, 130

Dorson, Richard, 61

Downing, Andrew Jackson, 82

"Drive-in society," 86

Duncanson, William Mayne, 72, 74, 148

Dutch, influence of on housing, 103-104. *See also* Cultural hearths, House types

Eagles Landing (Williamson, Georgia), 10

Easements, 14, 48, 51

Electricity: and appliances, 138; evidence of in housing, 37, 130; in lighting, 132; fittings for, 132; and motors, 132-133. *See also* Appliances, Rural Electrification Administration

Elite lists, 44

Encumbrances, 51

Engel, Jan Kristin, 91

English, influence of on housing, 97, 100-105. *See also* Cultural hearths, House types

Ethnicity: census documentation of, 56; impact of on housing, 97, 99, 107; documented in oral histories, 61; reflected in community, 1, 15. *See also* Cultural hearths, House types

Fachwerk, 103

Fair Housing Act of 1968, 91

False seaming, 27

Family, history, 2, 42; size, 24, 55, 135, 139; status, 56, 136, 139, 140, 150; structure, 39, 135, 141

Farmhouses: designed by Andrew Jackson Downing, 82; Hilly Grove as example of, 62; as part of landscape, 11, 17; New England, 138; post offices in, 56; utilities provided to, 127

Farm land, 13, 56. *See also* Landscape

Farms: abandoned, 17; Hilly Grove as case study of, 62-64; landscape features of, 10, 18; as status symbols, 140; as workplaces, 136

Federal Highway Act of 1956, 10, 91. *See also* automobile, Transportation

Federal Housing Authority (FHA), 87. *See also* government

Federal style architecture. *See* Architectural styles

Federal Writers Project, 41

Fences, 10, 15

Financing of housing, 83, 85, 92, 142

Finns, influence of on housing, 103. *See also* Cultural hearths, House types

Fire department logs. *See* Public records

Fireplaces. *See* Heating systems

517 E. Capitol St. (Washington, D.C.), as case study, 147-158

Fleming, Dolores A., 35

Flemish, influence of on housing, 103. *See also* Cultural hearths, House types

Floors, 34-36, 121

Folk housing, 107. *See also* House types

Folklore, 61, 105

"Forty-Niners," 106